PRAISE FOR *DELIBERATE OPTIMISM*

This book reminds us that w

ealize. The refreshing and encouraging perspective help and offers concrete actions and introspective suggestion: ficacy as professionals. By heeding the message, we can become empowered to do whatever we can to make a difference with our students, in our classrooms, and throughout our schools. It affirms that "can-do" attitude and culture that I witness in the National Forum's Schools to Watch middle-grades initiative across the country. The message of *Deliberate Optimism* reinforces my personal coping strategy of humming "Keep on the Sunny Side" when I encounter negativity and challenges!

—Deborah Kasak, EdD, executive director, National Forum to Accelerate
Middle-Grades Reform Schools to Watch Initiative

The monologue about teachers has been pretty awful over the past few years. Teachers did not get into the profession to be kicked around during political campaigns—they got into education because of a love for children and a passion for learning. *Deliberate Optimism* is for all of those teachers who have lost or forgotten that along the way. Read this book . . . and regain your optimism.

—Peter DeWitt, independent consultant, Finding Common Ground
by *Education Week,* Corwin author, and consulting editor for
the Corwin Connected Educators Series

Teaching is tough, but it's not supposed to be masochistic. Sometimes teachers forget that taking care of ourselves is an important part of the job. *Deliberate Optimism* helps educators learn how refill our mental and emotional gas tanks—or at least increase our fuel efficiency.

—Roxanna Elden, author, *See Me After Class: Advice for Teachers by Teachers*

Students have a right to see someone in the front of the room who is confident, competent, and incurably optimistic. Too often, the status quo in classrooms and buildings is decidedly—and powerfully—negative. Every district leader and building principal should put this book in the hands of teachers and teacher assistants—and then model the kind of deliberate optimism teachers have a right to expect from their leaders.

—Ron Nash, presenter and author of *The Active Classroom* series

This book is a must-have resource for experienced as well as novice teachers. Easy to read and implement, it offers a wealth of sensible, realistic, and inspiring advice about how to successfully manage the daily business of being a classroom teacher. Its positive message is simply empowering!

—Julia G. Thompson, author, *The First-Year Teacher's Survival Guide*

A must read for every educator. This book details why they must work to maintain their optimism and how they can do that—and does this with a twist of humor.

Nothing important can be accomplished without optimism. Since teaching is a task of highest importance, this book should be read by anyone who is, or aspires to be, a teacher.

In an era of relentless criticism and overriding pessimism about our educational system, this book will lift the spirits of all who work in schools.

—Michael Connolly, co-author, *Young Enough to Change the World*

With so much negativity heaped on education today, there is a need for sources of inspiration and this book provides it. Not only is the book a singular call to arms for teachers to reclaim their joy, but within these pages are real strategies for healing our souls and growing positive, nurturing classrooms. Bravo, my friends, we needed this book!

—Kevin Honeycutt, international speaker, author,
song writer, and program developer, Educational Services
and Staff Development Association of Central Kansas

Deliberate Optimism: Reclaiming the Joy in Education is a highly relevant and engaging book that goes directly to the heart and soul of what education should be, not what it has come to be. The authors offer practical suggestions on how to reclaim what we have lost in the struggle to keep students, learning, and relationships at the core of educational practice. Their suggestions provide a pathway for educators to take deliberate personal action to reject the increasingly dehumanizing and deadening effects of politicization and corporatization of education. *Deliberate Optimism* provides us with hope that the joy in education, which attracted us to our profession, is still available; it is just waiting for each of us to take deliberate action to reclaim it.

—Martin Tadlock, vice president and provost, Bemidji State University, MN

The authors have a realistic view of a teacher's daily life and provide realistic solutions for teachers to embrace optimism and positivity in a myriad of situations.

—Kati Searcy, teacher, Mountain Park Elementary School, GA

This book is a nice synthesis of current research and classic literature about climate, culture, and the environmental context of the classroom and the teachers' lounge.

—Chris Hubbuch, principal, Excelsior Springs Middle School, MO

The universe provides. Debbie asked me to review this book at a time when I was facing new and daunting challenges both at home and the workplace. *Deliberate Optimism* offers not only encouragement, but much more importantly, practical steps for maintaining and rebuilding realistic optimism at work, home, wherever. The authors' insights are grounded in the real world of too little funding, too much criticism, too many demands, too little time, etc. And they show how to find and nurture light there.

—Paul D. Deering, professor of education, University of Hawaii at Manoa

This is such an important book for every classroom teacher. I wish schools would keep a copy in the faculty room so teachers can get practical ideas for finding the fun in working with students! I love how the book provides deliberate strategies that help teachers overcome the everyday bumps in the road that accompany the classroom. Thank you Debbie, Jack, and Judith for reminding us that teaching kids should be joyful!

—Jared Covili, author, *Going Google: Powerful Tools for 21st Century Learning*

Justice and self-improvement are interdependent. You can't change yourself without working to change your world, and you can't change your world without working to change yourself. With realistic scenarios, clear, sympathetic suggestions, and funny offhand pop-culture references, Debbie Silver and her co-authors help educators tackle the latter half of this interdependence in *Deliberate Optimism*. In this book we are offered tools to cultivate the fund of energy and creativity we all need to set in motion real change.

—Dina Strasser, educator and author of http://theline.edublogs.org

Blind optimism is no more effective than blind pessimism when it applied to providing children a good education. Thankfully, respected educators Silver, Berckemeyer, and Baenen offer optimism as a tool with eyes wide open. While acknowledging the challenges—social, political, and professional—of today's teachers, the authors describe and promote concrete strategies for building, sustaining, and using optimistic behaviors to improve professional effectiveness. A great book for whole-school discussion—or to read simply for personal uplift—*Deliberate Optimism* belongs on every teacher and administrator's bookshelf—and hearts.

—Doug Johnson, author, *Teaching Outside the Lines*,
director of media and technology, Mankato Area Public Schools, MN

This book provides a framework for taking responsibility in classrooms, choosing to see the positives, dealing with problems rather than dwelling on them, recognizing that choices are always available, and building relationships with all in the school community.

—Charla Buford Bunker, literacy specialist, Great Falls High School, MT

Deliberate Optimism: Reclaiming the Joy in Education is a timely and important book. And imagine that—the pairing of the words "joy" and "education." That's as rare these days as the pairing of "productive" and "Congress."

In an era when teachers are the problem and children are raw material for some grim manufacturing process, this book is a refreshing antidote. Children and education should and can be joyful, unless we allow all the joy to be leached from our schools by the dreadful pessimists who get all the airtime, gnashing their teeth over test scores and proposing damaging "reforms."

Silver, Berckemeyer, and Baenen offer a Road to Joy (sorry, Beethoven). Every teacher and administrator should take this trip.

—Steve Nelson, head, Calhoun School

Deliberate Optimism

Reclaiming the Joy in Education

Debbie Silver

Jack C. Berckemeyer

Judith Baenen

FOR INFORMATION:

Corwin

A SAGE Company

2455 Teller Road

Thousand Oaks, California 91320

(800) 233-9936

www.corwin.com

SAGE Publications Ltd.

1 Oliver's Yard

55 City Road

London EC1Y 1SP

United Kingdom

SAGE Publications India Pvt. Ltd.

B 1/I 1 Mohan Cooperative Industrial Area

Mathura Road, New Delhi 110 044

India

SAGE Publications Asia-Pacific Pte. Ltd.

3 Church Street

#10-04 Samsung Hub

Singapore 049483

Executive Editor: Arnis Burvikovs

Associate Editor: Desirée A. Bartlett

Editorial Assistant: Ariel Price

Production Editor: Melanie Birdsall

Copy Editor: Lana Todorovic-Arndt

Typesetter: C&M Digitals (P) Ltd.

Proofreader: Annie Lubinsky

Indexer: Molly Hall

Cover Designer: Scott Van Atta

Marketing Manager: Lisa Lysne

Copyright © 2015 by Corwin

Printed in the United States of America

A catalog record of this book is available from the Library of Congress.

ISBN: 978-1-4833-0783-1

This book is printed on acid-free paper.

16 17 18 10 9 8 7 6 5 4

Contents

Preface

Deliberate Optimism: Reclaiming the Joy in Education is a book for anyone involved in education. It is written by three lifelong educators who cumulatively have taught almost every kind of student at every grade level.

Whether you are a beginning PreK teacher, a veteran high school department chair, a school leader, or anyone in between, you will find inspiration for doing what you currently do as well as positive, pragmatic steps you can take to build or maintain a sense of autonomy, competence, and relevance in your role.

Each chapter covers a different aspect of maintaining optimism in an educational setting. Through research-based strategies, practical examples, and thought-provoking scenarios, the authors provide food for thought along with enough humor to make the journey fun. Discussion questions and action steps follow each chapter, and an appendix of further activities is provided at the end of the book.

Chapter 1, Choosing to Become a Teacher Is a Telling Vote for Optimism, outlines the Five Principles of Deliberate Optimism, provides a rationale for each, and gives examples of how they work in actual practice. This chapter frames the foundation for the rest of the book.

> ## Essentials for Happiness
>
> - *Something to love*
> - *Something to do*
> - *Something to hope for*
>
> —Author unknown

Chapter 2, I'm Not an Optimist, but Hopefully, One Day I Will Be, explains the basic concept of optimism, what it is and what it is not. It describes a model for deliberately maintaining our positive view on events that are beyond our control.

Chapter 3, "But We Have This ONE Teacher Who Keeps Ruining Things for Everyone!" examines differences in learning styles, extrovert/introvert tendencies, and generational differences to help better understand ourselves and how we can interact more positively with colleagues.

Chapter 4, Building Healthy Relationships and an Optimistic Shared Community, considers the thorny issue of dealing with colleagues who are dysfunctional and/or who drain your spirit. Tips are provided for building a positive shared community.

Chapter 5, Creating the Optimistic Classroom: Building a Relationship Culture, explores the importance of joy and optimism as it relates to the most important aspect of education—the students—by building positive relationships with them. Fostering healthy interactions among students is also discussed.

Chapter 6, Reclaiming the Joy in Our Classrooms and Our Curriculum, summarizes how teachers can restore and maintain joy in their individual classrooms not only through engaging activities, but also by personalizing their domains.

Chapter 7, Balancing Your Life to Promote Optimism, reflects on what personal responsibility and choices have to do with our overall optimism. With both humor and fact the authors highlight the importance of taking care of oneself.

Chapter 8, Joyful School Communities: The Sum of Their Parts, looks at what administrators, parents, and local communities can do to help restore optimism and hope in our nation's schools as well as what teachers can do beyond their own classrooms.

Readers of this book will

- Be able to employ purposeful, intentional strategies to maintain a sense of optimism about their work

- Receive valuable insights on dealing with differing and/or difficult people in the profession

- Understand the importance of maintaining one's sense of self as well as one's health

- Obtain valuable ideas for fostering a positive school community

Acknowledgments

SPECIAL THANKS

Thanks to Jack Berckemeyer and Judith Baenen for their unwavering support of kids, of education, and of me. You are two of the funniest (but serious-about-kids-minded) people I know, and my life is better because you're in it.

—Debbie Silver

A special thanks to my coauthors, Debbie Silver and Judith Baenen. Thanks also to Lawrence Silver for his patience as Debbie worked long hours. On a personal note, my thanks to Jason Altamirano for teaching me the meaning of Deliberate Optimism.

—Jack C. Berckemeyer

Many thanks to my optimistic coauthors, Jack and Debbie, and to students everywhere who keep me *keeping on*—especially Josie, Ellie, and Gabby.

—Judith Baenen

We are most appreciative of the support we have had from Corwin, particularly our editors, Arnis Burvikovs and Desirée Bartlett. You made this book possible and the journey a lot easier.

—Debbie, Jack, and Judith

PUBLISHER'S ACKNOWLEDGMENTS

Corwin would like to thank the following reviewers for their editorial insight and guidance:

Charla Buford Bunker, Literacy Specialist
Great Falls High School
Sun River, MT

About the Authors

 **Debbie Silver,** retired teacher, speaker, author, and humorist, is an advocate for teachers and for students. She taught for over 30 years as a classroom teacher, teacher leader, and university professor. Along the way, she taught nearly every grade level and nearly every kind of student. She wrote the best-selling books *Drumming to the Beat of Different Marchers* and *Fall Down 7 Times, Get Up 8: Teaching Kids to Succeed.* This award-winning former Louisiana State Teacher of the Year now lives in Texas and travels throughout the United States and abroad working with those who want to improve education.

 **Jack C. Berckemeyer,** author, presenter, consultant, and humorist, is from Denver, Colorado. He was a classroom teacher and worked for the National Middle School Association (currently AMLE) as the assistant executive director for 13 years and now is the owner of Berckemeyer Consulting Group. He runs the Nuts and Bolts Ready to Lead, Teach and Learn Symposiums and works with schools all over the world. He is the author of *Managing the Madness* and *Taming of the Team* and coauthor of *H.E.L.P for Teachers* with Judith Baenen.

 **Judith Baenen** is an international speaker and consultant focusing on the middle grades. She was a classroom teacher, headmaster of an independent school, and former director of member services for the National Middle School Association (AMLE). She is the author of AMLE's best-selling pamphlets, *H.E.L.P.* and *More H.E.L.P.,* and she coauthored *H.E.L.P. for Teachers* with Jack Berckemeyer. For several years, she was editor of AMLE's *Family Connection.* Her humorous presentations and workshops centering on young adolescent development and engaging families with schools have made her a popular speaker throughout the United States and on almost every continent. (She's still waiting for a call from Antarctica.)

This book is dedicated to our families and friends who support us unconditionally and to our fellow educators who still believe that what they do matters.

Introduction

Your profession is not what brings home your weekly paycheck, your profession is what you're put here on earth to do, with such passion and such intensity that it becomes spiritual in calling.

—Vincent van Gogh

We believe that despite the recent onslaught of criticism leveled at teachers and the negative lens through which some of the media have chosen to view our vocation, teaching is still the most noble profession. What other group of people have more power to shape the future by empowering the next generation to think, to create, and to act compassionately toward their fellow man?

We are grateful for our respective journeys in the field of education, and we are adamant about encouraging positive, effective people to join the ranks of educators who still believe we can make significant differences for learners. However, it is becoming difficult to attract competent candidates to the teaching profession and even harder to retain them. In the United States, teacher turnover approximates 20 percent each year, with higher rates for new teachers and in urban areas. Student achievement levels and district budgets are severely impacted by the rising turnover in teacher educators.

In our work with teachers, particularly in the United States, we are witnessing a dismaying decline in their feelings of status and power. A general feeling of helplessness and futility seems to be growing among educators as the public perception of schools reaches new lows. In light of the escalating focus on a never-ending plethora of standardized assessments and newly minted teacher evaluations, educators tell us they have lost their zest for teaching—that special spark that ignites their passion for their particular disciplines and for their students. Administrators tell us they sense a general loss of joy in classrooms as curriculums are defined, scripted, and monitored by those far removed from the classroom.

We do not mean to imply that there are no longer "pockets of excellence" across the nation where both students and teachers embrace their learning institutions as places that are safe, engaging, and generally happy. Each of us can point to schools that offer the best kinds of learning environments for students and are appreciated by the adults who work there as well as the communities they serve. We hope that every school is working to grow toward that kind of quality.

Because exemplary schools are not universal, however, there are policy makers, community members, administrators, parents, and even teachers who have allowed themselves to get caught in the *blame game* in which pointing fingers gets priority over working on solutions. And because most of the pointed fingers of late have been directed at classrooms, some teachers quite understandably have taken a defensive posture as well as defeatist attitude. This negativity helps no one, and as one of our authors likes to say, "We are done with that!"

Together we decided to write a book about how we as educators can take back our power, our joy, and our optimism. For every teacher, the journey to this profession is a complex and unique road. We believe the amazing adventure of teaching is a calling, and it requires ongoing purpose and effort to sustain its viability. We three authors grew up in different parts of the country and taught in vastly diverse school settings, and we each have our own areas of expertise. Nonetheless, we have been friends and colleagues for over two decades, and we share a common belief that a sense of humor, an awareness of personal responsibility, a commitment to purpose, and a feeling of realistic optimism are the keys to sustained fulfillment in this profession.

We do not intend this book to be a giant infomercial about unrealistic cheerfulness. (You will not asked to purchase a boxed CD collection of our favorite happy tunes, pressured to make a donation to the Just-Turn-That-Frown-Upside-Down Foundation, or be coerced into signing up for a daily e-mail reminder of how much better you have it than the pioneers did.) We understand that no amount of chest pounding, fire walking, or repeating mantras will have teachers saying things like:

> "You're here for an unscheduled supervisory visit from the State Department? No worries. I always like my merit pay observation to be made in my last period class on the day before spring break."

> "I'm sure there's an excellent reason they are resurfacing our parking lot the day before school starts. I'll just park in the muddy field three blocks away and make six or seven trips to unload my car. The exercise will be good for me."

> "Johnny, you just fed a box of crayons to the class hamster? Well, look at you—you've just provided me with a learning moment to teach about the alimentary canal."

Probably that kind of levity can only be induced by heavy use of pharmaceuticals, and we are not recommending that (yet). Nevertheless, we believe there are many things educators can do to alleviate some of the basic annoyances as well as the overt and covert challenges we face daily.

In *Deliberate Optimism: Reclaiming the Joy in Education*, we endeavor to help school leaders and their teachers regain a sense power and influence. We believe that a candid examination of how we educators are sometimes our own worst enemy will help us as a group to stop "shooting ourselves in the foot" and start speaking in a collective voice that will be heard. We want our profession to regain its moral calling and teachers to reclaim their joy in doing their jobs.

We respectfully (and sometimes tongue-in-cheek) submit our ideas for our brothers and sisters in the *educationnation*.

CHAPTER 1

Choosing to Become a Teacher Is a Telling Vote for Optimism

Optimism is the foundation of all good teaching. Optimism in the face of daunting reality is downright heroic—and that, in fact, is what good teachers practice all day long while others denigrate their contributions to society.

—Rafe Esquith (2014)

When we (the authors) write about optimism, we do not intend to imply that teachers should show up every day with perpetual grins pasted on their faces. Nor are we talking about educators doing cartwheels down the hall to face an angry parent in the office, or dancing gleefully into a required professional development meeting on blood-borne pathogens, or squealing with delight when given the task of disaggregating student data from the latest high-stakes test results. Just as with any job or profession, we all have duties that are less than pleasant. Our intent is to examine realistic, purposeful strategies teachers and school leaders can employ to restore their hope in a system they feel is rapidly heading off course.

When individuals decide to become teachers, they enter an unbreakable pact with the future. They promise to do the best they can with what they have and with what they know in order to mold successfully the next generation. As educators, we know that it is our obligation to grow, to learn, and to reflect on how to improve ourselves every year so that we leave the future of this world in the best, most capable, most educated hands imaginable. If we don't subscribe to this noble purpose, then what are we doing in education?

Five Principles of Deliberate Optimism for Educators

> *An outstanding principal we know walks into the school cafeteria every day and shouts, "Whose school is this?" The students and teachers respond loudly, "Our school!" Building optimism means believing in our philosophy, "Our School, Our Team, Our Kids!"*

We realize that the challenges of teaching today are greater than they have ever been before. Schools have become a political minefield of mandated policies and procedures that censure original thinking and creative innovation. Teachers are expected to address standards-based instruction (SBI), Common Core Curriculum (CCC), response to intervention (RTI), end-of-course assessment (EOC), positive behavior intervention and supports (PBIS), and problem-based learning (PBL) in their classrooms. We are asked to participate in professional learning communities (PLCs) for part of our professional development activities (PDs). We must learn to separate student data gleaned from standardized tests, design plans for differentiated instruction (D.I.), and focus on the multiple intelligences (M.I.) of each child. In our classrooms, we now have students on medication, students who *need* to be on medication, students who don't speak our language, students who sleep in cars at night, students who don't get to be kids when they go home from school, and students who would rather be anywhere else than at school. We have kids who endure more heartache in a month than many of us will have to confront in a lifetime. And sometimes, we also teach kids who will never have to work a day in their lives and are already acting like it.

The sheer number of problems in teaching may sometimes seem insurmountable. Rather than being overwhelmed by circumstances, though, we think there are some concrete practical steps that will help teachers remain hopeful no matter what the adversity. Influenced by the works of some of the world's greatest optimists, Dale Carnegie, Norman Vincent Peale, Martin Seligman, Stephen Covey, and others, we developed the Five Principles for Deliberate Optimism for educators. We use them throughout this book to guide the discussion about how teachers, administrators, and other staff can intentionally and effectively become realistic optimists.

1. BEFORE ACTING OR *REACTING*, GATHER AS MUCH INFORMATION FROM AS MANY VARIED SOURCES AS POSSIBLE.

Perhaps because of the overscheduled, crazy busy lives most of us educators lead, we sometimes rely on others to articulate critical issues impacting our lives. We listen to our preferred news outlet with a naïve belief that it is imparting unbiased facts to us rather than trying to create or spin a story to increase ratings. We receive information about the latest legislative mandate filtered through

Five Principles of Deliberate Optimism

1. Before acting or *reacting,* **gather as much information** from as many varied sources as possible.

2. **Determine what is beyond your control** and strategize how to minimize its impact on your life.

3. **Establish what you can control** and seek tools and strategies to help you maximize your power.

4. Actively *do* **something positive** toward your goal.

5. **Take ownership** of your plan and acknowledge responsibility for your choices. ■

second-, third-, and fourth-party sources with their own agendas rather than reading the actual bill or proposal.

We have all been there. Someone returns from a district workshop with the news, "Get ready folks because *They* are completely doing away with cooperative learning! A lady in my group told me that her cousin's daughter, who is a teacher, said her principal mentioned that he heard it from a reliable source. *They* are going to prohibit the use of cooperative learning in all Common Core disciplines. It's true! From now on, we won't be allowed to let students work in groups. Can you believe that? Oh my gosh, I don't know what *They* are thinking! I cannot give up my groups. That's the only way I have ever taught. *Those people* are crazy. Most of them haven't been in a classroom in 30 years, and now *They* want to tell *Us* how to teach? I don't think so. That's the last straw for me. I'm going to turn in my resignation, buy a pair of skates, and go be a carhop for Sonic." And the word spreads like head lice. By the end of the day, everyone in your school is preoccupied with the new mandate (which of course, turns out to be completely untrue).

Throughout the book, we talk more about how to avoid this kind of negativism and provide ideas for better choices than just blindly following along or chiming in when problems occur. For now we want to highlight the point that each of us needs to make every effort to collect accurate information before we react to or act on hearsay.

We're not saying that schools, districts, states, and the federal Department of Education give every issue impartial treatment or that the decisions they make are always fair or even sensible. But we know from experience that it is vital for each of us involved to know as much as possible about impending issues. We need to be aware, realistic, and as informed as possible.

Realistic Awareness. Before we buy into or begin reacting to what is being disseminated as *the truth*, it is our responsibility to ask ourselves some guiding questions:

1. Who exactly is "*They?*" Are we talking about a person, a committee, a voting body, or some other entity? It's important to know exactly who is responsible for the alleged decision.

2. Have I done my own research/fact checking on the current education issue or topic?

3. Have I sought out and listened to at least two sides of the issue or topic?

4. Have I relied on the words of others to help form my opinion? If so, have I considered their possible biases and credibility?

5. Have I tried to separate the facts from my preconceptions about those who made the decision (including attributing motives based on my assumptions)?

6. Was there an opportunity for me or for other affected parties to voice our opinions about the matter before a decision was made?

7. Are we as a staff waiting to react, or are we looking to begin a proactive approach to the problem?

8. Have we looked closely at the data used to support the new mandate?

9. Have we made an effort to contact similar schools or districts that have already implemented this program?

10. Have we as a staff dissected the full potential impact (pros and cons) on ourselves, our school, our community, and most importantly, our students?

Reviewing and reflecting on these questions might take time, but in the long run, the process will encourage helpful deliberations and perhaps influence those around us to think carefully before drawing conclusions.

2. DETERMINE WHAT IS BEYOND YOUR CONTROL AND STRATEGIZE HOW TO MINIMIZE ITS IMPACT ON YOUR LIFE.

Nan Henderson (2013) correctly maintains, "Educators cannot eradicate poverty, remove neighborhood gangs, stop cultural violence, heal parental addictions, or prevent the myriad of other types of stress, risk, and trauma many students face daily" (p. 22). Likewise, we cannot as individuals stop widespread abuse, neglect, lack of parental support, debilitating health and learning disorders, or any manner of large scale cases of social injustice. We cannot control which students come to our schools and which ones leave. We do not get to decide how school or district resources are allocated. We don't even have the final say in what grade, discipline, or even what curriculum we will teach.

Job Placement. Of course, part of our job placement is determined by our degree(s) earned, our area(s) of certification, and perhaps even our experience in a particular area. Schools have to provide documentation to the state that we are qualified (and now "highly qualified" under the No Child Left Behind Act) for the job assignment we have. In emergencies, a teacher can teach out of field, but for the most part, certain certifications are required to teach in specific areas. We usually warn teacher candidates to be careful about the certifications they earn. If you have a certification to teach high school humanities, and somewhere along the way you also acquired a certification in PreK–K instruction, your district can compel you to teach a kindergarten class (even if you'd rather have a root canal sans painkillers than teach anyone below ninth grade). Tenure normally stipulates that you will have a job but not which job you will have. In some districts, teacher unions have negotiated a bit more individual power in job selection, but for the most part, when you are hired by a district, you have no legal right to say which school you prefer or what you will teach.

Curriculum. Sometimes individual teachers are misinformed about who has the right to dictate curriculum. It is the constitutional right of the states to decide what they want to be taught in their schools. Sometimes states allow individual districts to make decisions within the state framework, but it is basically the state's responsibility to oversee curriculum. Recently the federal government has interjected itself into curriculum decisions by tying monetary rewards and compensation to its desired curriculum requirements, but states and districts have the right to refuse the money and choose their own curriculums. For example, the CCC is strongly supported by the federal government, but as of this writing, Texas, Nebraska, Virginia, and Alaska have opted to write their own state curriculums. The point is that it is not up to teachers to decide what subject matter they are going to teach in their classroom. Standards and essential ideas are determined beyond the individual teacher's level; consequently, time spent wailing over curriculum choices to people who are not decision makers is wasted. Sometimes, there are long-term solutions in which a teacher can become involved (write letters, volunteer to serve on committees, talk to decision makers), but for the most part, like job placement, the decision is not ours to make.

It is our contention that while we support the states' right to determine curriculum and establish standards, we wholeheartedly support the individual teacher's right to determine how and when we teach the mandated curriculum. We talk more about that in Chapter 6. The upshot is that constantly wringing our hands over things we cannot change is a waste of time and one sure way to lose optimism. There are many things we can control, and those are the areas in which we need to focus our positive energy and our resources. One of the most important factors in reclaiming our optimism is to acknowledge those things we cannot control and go around them.

"Well, okay then." The Story of Mrs. Touhy

There are people who are able to put things into perspective and continue toward their goals no matter what the obstacles. The movie *The Blindside* tells the story of Michael Oher, now a famous football player for the 2013 Super Bowl winning Baltimore Ravens. It chronicles his life as a young African American raised in poverty and neglect who eventually is embraced, then adopted, by a conservative Caucasian family in Tennessee, the Touhys. Predictable obstacles occur throughout the story, but one of the things that inspires us is the manner in which Michaels's new guardian, Leigh Anne Touhy, meets each one. She listens closely, considers the problem, and gives the same answer each time, "Well, okay then." In other words, she tells Michael that she understands the obstacles, she hears what he is saying, and now she's ready to regroup and try another route.

It seems to us that a majority of teachers have long embraced Leigh Anne Touhy's "Well, okay then" philosophy. In spite of budget cuts, incomprehensible mandates, solutions-du-jour program adoptions, students who arrive at school ill-prepared and sometimes ill-cared for, and countless other challenges we face daily, the majority of teachers have always been able to evaluate the situation, consider all the factors, and start over with the attitude of Mrs. Touhy, "Well, okay then." It's not fun, and it's not happy. Perhaps the only way to sustain this kind of hopeful, down-to-business nature is to believe in the power of our influence, to trust in a larger purpose, and to have clearly defined long-term goals. Teachers have to believe that what we do matters and what we accomplish has meaning beyond short-term data aggregation and subjective judgments from those who have little or no idea about the components of effective education.

What we are talking about is not a goal of continual ecstasy, but rather an overarching hopefulness and confidence about the future successful outcomes of our efforts. The optimism we support is not some vague hope that eventually things will all work out, but rather a positive, realistic conviction that we have control over certain aspects of our jobs and no control over others. Most of us have a lot more power than we realize, and all of us can choose how we will react to those things we cannot control.

Cynicism is contagious; so is hope.

—Richard Curwin (2013)

We can throw up our hands and say, "I can't do this," or we can look challenge in the eye and say, "Well, okay then, I'll try it another way."

DELIBERATE OPTIMISM

Exercise

An elementary science teacher is assigned to teach hands-on science to third- to fifth-grade students. Her room is a temporary building standing alone in the middle of the playground. She has no reasonable access to running water. She tells her administrator that she needs available water in order to provide students with the hands-on experiences she wants them to have. She is told there is no budget for plumbing her room for water, so she will just have to work around the problem. "Well, okay then." What could she do? Think of as many practical solutions as you can. Be innovative. If you are in a book study group, stop here and brainstorm ideas before reading further. If you are reading this by yourself, stop just a minute and try to think of ideas before reading on. Seriously, stop reading until you have thought of at least three ideas. ■

But What If . . .

An ingenious teacher we know arranged with the school custodian to run a water hose with an attached spray nozzle from the closest outdoor spigot through one of her classroom windows and into a bucket in her classroom. On days she needed water, she turned on the outdoor faucet and left the nozzle closed until she needed water. She got a local store to donate large plastic tubs for basins, and all she had to do was squeeze the handle on the nozzle when she wanted to run water. Afterward, the students poured the noncontaminated water onto grass around the building. Both she and the students enjoyed having the water they needed to do the wonderfully messy activities she planned.

It would be easy to start picking this one solution apart. Sometimes negative people's knee jerk response to a creative solution is, "But what if . . . ?" Teachers in colder climates may ask what happens when it's freezing outside? Those located on the second floor of a building might dismiss the idea as too impractical for them. P.E. teachers might object to having a garden hose running across a playing field. Maybe the windows at your school don't open. All of those are valid objections, but forward-thinking teachers focus less on what won't work and spend more time on what will. When we are hamstrung with the idea of how awful it is for a teacher to be put in that situation in the first place, we stop seeking solutions. Teachers are the most creative, innovative, resourceful people we know (mainly because we *have* to be), and we believe our challenge as realistic optimists is to find what works in our particular situations. Once we have the most clear, realistic view of perceived obstacles, we need to give ourselves permission to move on from things beyond our control (and there are many of those).

Sometimes the things beyond our control are more than mere annoyances or inhibitive distracters. We are all aware of sporadic violence as well catastrophic geologic and weather events that have impacted schools. While these occurrences are devastating, we know that teachers are usually the first ones on the scene to help restore order and a sense of security for students. There are indeed circumstances where life just gets in the way of even our best plans. "Well, okay then." We need to pick up the pieces and move forward with what we are able to control.

3. ESTABLISH WHAT YOU CAN CONTROL AND SEEK TOOLS AND STRATEGIES TO HELP YOU MAXIMIZE YOUR POWER.

We believe that teachers have more power than they sometimes realize, and we wrote this book to support educators across the board in their quest to regain a sense of autonomy, competence, and relatedness. Chapter 2 concentrates on research about and strategies for empowering educators with a focus on what we can control, and every chapter will include tips and ideas for managing our choices and effort. It is true that we cannot change some of our least favorite things about our circumstances, but we can always change the way we deal with those circumstances.

It is our desire to present not only suggestions about how to reframe realistic optimism in education, but also to provide concrete steps for getting there. We have gathered ideas from educators across the country, and we want to share what they and we have found to be helpful in maintaining one's sense of efficacy in the classroom and beyond. Some ideas may be new, some may be a twist on classic ideas, and some may be iterations of things you already do (and isn't that always affirming?). Even though particular circumstances sometimes leave a teacher feeling isolated and alone, that does not have to be the case. As a whole, teachers are natural nurturers and selflessly reach out to one another when they are given the opportunity.

We live in an amazingly connected world that allows educators easy access to each other and to each other's resources. We encourage you to share your great ideas through appropriate Internet connections (blogs, listservs, Twitter, Pinterest, Instagram, or remarkable future programs yet to be designed). We are tremendous supporters of teachers attending conferences that deal with their grade groups and/or disciplines (both as presenters and as attendees). We believe it is extremely helpful for educators to join the professional organizations that provide us with journals, conferences, online support, and other valuable services.

We realize that as teachers, we are a vast and varied group. We teach different disciplines and age groups. Teachers work in urban schools, international schools, rural schools, online schools, public schools, private schools, as homebound teachers, in detention facilities, and in more situations than we can list. We have diverse (and sometimes *multiple*) personalities, talents, and experience levels. Some of the suggestions we offer may not work or even appeal to every reader. Some ideas may be something to put on hold and try later. Optimally, every reader will recognize those things within himself or herself that he or she can change to make his or her professional life more appealing and satisfying.

WHAT YOU CAN'T CONTROL	WHAT YOU CAN CONTROL
Curriculum—Usually decided by the state or local district	How you use the curriculum to engage students and lead them to success
Job placement—Guidelines provided by the local district	Learning everything you can about the grade-level and subject matter in order to ensure desired outcomes students achieve
Colleagues' attitudes—Some are worn down, worn out, or not meant to be in teaching.	Keep yourself healthy and upbeat. Use encouragement instead of argument.
Student context—Everything from neglected to overprotected	Make every day in your class a lesson in stability and thoughtful decision making.
Parent expectations—The best for their child, but sometimes unreasonable	Communicate with parents in every way possible. Build relationships.

4. ACTIVELY *DO* SOMETHING POSITIVE TOWARD YOUR GOAL.

Dale Carnegie once said, "Action breeds confidence and courage. If you want to conquer fear, do not sit home and think about it. Go out and get busy." We are all familiar with the term "paralyzed by fear." But in addition to fear, other factors can stop a person from acting—a sense of helplessness, a sense of hopelessness, frustration, fatigue, disillusionment, anger, revenge, not knowing where to start, a feeling of being overwhelmed, a sense of futility. There are many reasons teachers stop acting in the best interest of their students. Some are valid, but none are acceptable.

How many of us have had or have known teachers who retired long before they left the classroom? Administrators, too, sometimes meet various challenges with words like, "Well, I'm going to be retiring in 2 years anyway." If we (the authors) were independently wealthy people, we would pay those folks to go home now because we know not much positive is happening for the students under their care. No matter what the cause, inaction can lead to fatalism, complacency, inattention, negativity, pessimism, isolationism, and boredom. Inaction is a clear signal that the person is no longer willing to take a risk or learn anything new. If we don't take action, we fail by default and can't even learn from the experience.

For that reason, we believe that it is not enough merely to want to improve or to waste time rationalizing how the system has made it impossible to do our jobs. The best and most productive approach is to *do* something—anything we think is in the best interest of our ultimate purpose. Even if we make a mistake, actually doing something brings with it a certain kind of strength. Making a plan, sticking to it, and analyzing the results is energy restoring. Teachers need to remember that maybe we can't do everything for kids, but we can do *something*. It's fine to start

> We may not always be able to reach every student, but we must reach for every student.
>
> —Scott Sater, teacher, Shakopee, MN

small. Reach out to just one child. Or try a new teaching strategy with just one class. The point is to start. Doing challenging tasks brings a sense of excitement as well as a sense of accomplishment.

There is a kind of inertia involved in action. Inaction tends to reinforce itself with more inactivity. On the other hand, action tends to invigorate individuals and perpetuate more action. Effective educators accept that obstacles may slow us down, but they will not stop us. We are the only ones who can stop ourselves permanently. The best way to move toward our purpose is decisively to do those things we can to help our students and our fellow educators.

In writing an article about how educators can rejuvenate themselves during the summer months, Debbie Silver (2013b) writes,

> Plan something new for next school year. Focus on something novel for the upcoming school session. Think about a positive aspect of your job you want to enhance or rebuild or something you have been wanting to try. Pick a project that reignites your enthusiasm for teaching and direct your efforts towards something you can look forward to. (p. 18)

> The things we take for granted . . . the rock solid things that make up our confidence will change. The change will make us stronger, or it will drive us from our chosen endeavor.
>
> —Joe Bishop, Wyoming educator

In other words, the best way we can revive our spirits is to focus on something we can control and deliberately enact steps to empower ourselves toward that end.

5. TAKE OWNERSHIP OF YOUR PLAN AND ACKNOWLEDGE RESPONSIBILITY FOR YOUR CHOICES.

As presenters, the three of us consistently remind educators and educational entities that teachers need more of a voice. We encourage teachers to stand up and be heard. More and more we see teacher-generated blogs and articles and listen to teacher presenters who advocate for a larger teacher presence in important decision making. After all, who is there better to speak about what works best for kids than the people on the frontlines in the classrooms every school day? But in order for this to happen, we the educators have to be willing to stop blaming outside factions and bickering among ourselves. We need to acknowledge our collective weaknesses and bring to the forefront our combined strengths. (Maybe it is time to stop worrying about who took our *clearly labeled personal* yogurt out of the lounge refrigerator or parked in our favorite parking spot and start dealing with the real issues.)

It is time we are more honest with ourselves and with each other. We realize that educators will confront parents, students, and even their administrators (as long as two people come with them), but most are afraid to confront a coworker. We sometimes prefer to "let sleeping dogs lie" than to speak up. Rather than uniformly going along when one of our colleagues is out of line, we should stand up for what we think is ethically correct.

Scenario: Hall Duty

Think about the teacher who never is at her door during class change. She finds countless excuses for why she cannot manage to make her way to the hall, even though the administrator has repeatedly told teachers to make it a priority to be there. You and some of the other teachers have complained among yourselves more than once about having to "pick up her slack." Inevitably the administrator is in the hall during a class change, and she's not at her door. He asks you and a couple of other teachers if this is her normal behavior. You hedge and reply, "We really haven't noticed." The principal walks into her room, discusses the incident, and tells her he is going to put a note of reprimand in her file. Immediately, she is in the hall in tears wanting to be consoled by her comrades. What do you do?

A. Hug her, dry her tears, and tell her what a horrible, terrible, no good, very bad person the principal is.

B. Assure her that everyone skips hall duty occasionally, and it was just bad luck she got caught.

C. Offer to find a way to alert her the next time an administrator is in the hall.

D. Tell her that you're sorry she got a reprimand, but there are several reasons she should be in the hall.

E. Nod politely and walk away quickly. ∎

Of course the best thing for everyone is answer "D." All the adults at school need to support one another, but also, we need to hold each other accountable. Even with adults, positive peer pressure is a compelling impetus for influencing behavior. We don't want to be complicit in allowing the adults at school to do less than their best. Perhaps you and the other teachers could share tips on how you make the time to be at the door during class change. You could express your feelings or even offer research about the importance of the teacher greeting each child as he or she enters the room. We teachers need to challenge each other to do our very best for students in every possible way.

Taking ownership of our profession means that we stop excusing, stop blaming, and start taking responsibility. We make decisions based on what is best for students, and we behave with an integrity grounded in a shared value-system. We avoid blame because we know it subverts personal growth and makes us victims instead of visionaries.

We need to be honest about constraining forces beyond our control and realistic about what we can do. We ought to acknowledge our shortcomings, learn from our experiences (both good and bad), and purposefully get better at what we do. Taking responsibility means we make decisions and live with the outcomes. We learn from our mistakes and move on.

We as teachers need to step up and take responsibility for not only our own classrooms but for every student in our schools. We need to be willing to offer guidance to novice colleagues, work with teachers who are struggling, and learn from teachers more accomplished than we. It is time to let those few incompetent, ineffective colleagues know that we are moving forward, and they can join us or get out of the way. We need to listen to parents, community members, and other interested parties with an open mind and an open heart. In addition, we need to let them know we are qualified, competent, skilled professionals who are responsible for decisions we make about our classrooms.

Upon the retirement of 35-year veteran kindergarten teacher, Lil Lufkin, her head of school at Calhoun School in Manhattan, Steven Nelson, wrote the following tribute letter:

Dear Lil,

Thirty five years, 15 kids—give or take—to a class. That makes 525 kids you have loved and taught. You've spent about 50,400 hours teaching during those 35 years. That's enough time to visit Pluto and return, yet you have stayed in one place. Remarkable.

During this, your final year of teaching, rock stars have been idolized, athletes have signed multimillion dollar contracts before they are old enough to vote and business leaders have been convicted because of shabby ethics and practices. They have been in *The New York Times* and you have not. You have stayed in one place, teaching children while controversy swirled over the war in Vietnam, while the Hubble Telescope captured breathtaking pictures of the infant universe, and while the Dow Jones Industrial average went from 750 to 12,000. You have stayed in one place, teaching children, while Elvis died and reappeared in small towns everywhere, while the Berlin Wall fell, and while the nation enjoyed unprecedented prosperity and endured unspeakable terror.

A lot happened while you were just sitting around in one place teaching children!

There is no profession as important as teaching children and you have done it with rare grace, skill, good humor, and abundant love. You should be the *Time* magazine Woman of the Year. You should win multiple Oscars, Tonys, and Emmys. You should be awarded the Pulitzer Prize for Niceness and the Nobel Prize for Dedication. But you won't. Teachers don't become household names unless they do something really awful and all you have done are really wonderful things.

Yes, you have taught long enough to visit Pluto and return, yet you have stayed in one place. Some people travel to far galaxies and other people prepare them for the trip. For 35 years you have been Calhoun's NASA. You have inspired and cajoled, taught and hugged. You have given your hundreds of kids a confident and unconditionally affirming start and sewn their flight jackets with threads of wisdom and joy. You've laughed at their 5-year old jokes and been gob-smacked by their insights. You've wiped their noses (and behinds) and put smiles back on their faces just when they needed it. And because of you, 525 kids believed they could travel to the stars or accomplish anything they wished. And they have. And they will.

There can be no life achievement greater than to have affected the lives of 525 humans in a profound and irreversible way. In any other context this statement might be trite, but in your case it is irrefutably true: You have changed the world for the better.

SOURCE: Nelson (2013).

Action Steps for Teachers

DISCUSSION QUESTIONS AND ACTIVITIES

1. Think back on all the factors that influenced you to become a teacher. Describe to the group both the positive and negative forces that influenced you as you moved toward the job you have now. (See "Life on a Roll" activity in the Appendix, page 138.)

2. Describe the most optimistic teacher you ever had or presently know. List the qualities about that person that led you to believe she or he had a positive view of life. What distinguished that person from other teachers? How did (do) you feel when you were (are) around her or him?

3. List the factors that you think presently deter teachers from feeling optimistic. Has your optimism suffered a hit recently? Why or why not?

4. Where do you get the majority of your information about school? What about the information on the world in general? Do you think your source(s) influences the way you feel about things? Do you think other people's source(s) of information influence their attitudes about things? If so, in what ways?

5. Pick a current hot issue at school. Use the steps in "Realistic Awareness" (Appendix, page 139) to further explore the topic. Did using the steps expand your ideas about the subject? Why or why not?

6. Think of a school problem you are currently dealing with. Brainstorm as many creative solutions as you can (don't edit yourself or limit yourself to traditional ideas). Discuss each proposed solution and decide if it would be worth trying.

7. Do you think it is hard to be honest with colleagues about their choices and actions? Why or why not?

8. List three uncontrollable issues affecting your school that bother you. Estimate the amount of time you and others at your school worry or talk about them weekly. What are some ways you can *go around* the issues and keep moving forward?

Action Steps for School Leaders

1. Plan a staff meeting to introduce and/or reinforce the Five Principles of Deliberate Optimism. Lead a group in using the five principles to deal with a schoolwide issue. (You can use "The Five Principles of Deliberate Optimism" worksheet found in the Appendix, page 140, to give participants a place to start.)

2. Acquaint parents and the community with the Five Principles of Deliberate Optimism by adding the principles to school newsletters and other school publications as well as discussing them in parent-teacher organization, parent-teacher association, or similar meetings.

3. Have the Five Principles of Deliberate Optimism printed for every staff member. You can use laminated pocket cards, squeeze balls, posters, or whatever suits the style of your school community.

4. Use funny and/or motivating video clips to begin faculty meetings. Never miss an opportunity to affirm the great things staff members do for the kids and for the school.

5. Fight for time for teachers to meet informally, reflect, and grow professionally. Encourage teachers to select their own areas for growth and assist them in getting the appropriate professional development opportunities they need.

6. Delegate more responsibility to teacher leaders. Allow them to work with small groups to discuss both major and minor issues affecting student learning. Acknowledge their contributions and try to utilize as many of their suggestions as possible.

7. When there is a problem (e.g., teachers arriving late for duty assignments), speak directly to those responsible. Blanket e-mails or general announcements at faculty meetings are usually ignored by the transgressors and are demoralizing to those who are doing what they are supposed to do.

8. At ball games or at other extracurricular activities, make an announcement asking teachers and staff to stand and be recognized. Let others know about their added effort.

9. Surprise your teachers by taking something off their plates instead of adding to them. Find something teachers are required to do that is not really that important or a program that hasn't been all that successful and announce that you are striking that procedure or program. They will love you for it.

10. Ask teachers to give you a list of things you and your administrative staff can do to make their jobs easier. The requests can be signed or anonymous. Do as many as you can and try to acknowledge the ones you cannot do. (For example, at a faculty meeting you might state, "I'd like to acknowledge the request I got from one of you to limit the number of students in each of your sections to 24. Unfortunately, with our present number of students and teachers that is not possible, but I'm willing to look at a more equitable way to balance classes if you'll write me or come by my office and give me more details about your particular situation." Or, "I'd like to acknowledge the request for me to take a long walk off a short pier, but I really need you to be a bit more specific about what is bothering you.")

CHAPTER 2

I'm Not an Optimist, but Hopefully, One Day I Will Be

I am fundamentally an optimist. Whether that comes from nature or nurture, I cannot say. Part of being optimistic is keeping one's head pointed toward the sun, one's feet moving forward. There were many dark moments when my faith in humanity was sorely tested, but I would not and could not give myself up to despair. That way lays defeat and death.

—Nelson Mandela, *Long Walk to Freedom: Autobiography of Nelson Mandela* (1995)

Is optimism a product of nature or nurture? We believe that one's disposition may be influenced by nature, but a state of optimism can be developed and maintained by anyone who chooses to frame his or her perceptions in a manner that is both realistic and positive. This chapter examines the ideology of optimism as it applies to educators and provides a specific model for reframing thoughts.

There are those who believe that people are either born with optimistic tendencies or they are not. Some people are told, "You have always been a happy person. Even as a baby you were such a cheerful little thing." Or a person might overhear a parent say, "He was a cranky, finicky infant, and he hasn't changed a bit. It's like living with Oscar the Grouch. He could find a way to depress Richard Simmons." Perhaps you know a student or an adult whose natural facial expression is a frown. Maybe you attribute this negative persona to something within the person that cannot be changed. We do not agree. There is a reason we like to use the term *deliberate optimism*. We believe it can be learned, developed, and maintained. We do acknowledge that some people seem to be more outwardly cheerful than others, but we strongly argue that anyone can deliberately change his or her attitude.

Many educators believe that it is getting harder and harder to make the best of their tough situations. Well-known educator/author Rafe Esquith writes about a teacher he sees frowning one Friday afternoon. When he asks her why she is grumpy on a Friday of all days, she replies, "It just means Monday is that much closer." He concedes that being optimistic is sometimes difficult:

> . . . A teacher works hard all day, comes home, and reads an article blaming him or her for the failure of students to do well on tests or behave appropriately. I don't know the exact moment when teachers became the scapegoat for factors beyond their control, but the moment has come. And the unfair, often ridiculous expectations being placed on teachers explain why some of them can't even be happy about an upcoming weekend of family and fun, knowing that Monday looms. (2014, p. 20)

Though we don't dispute Mr. Esquith's point about the pessimistic perceptions and unreasonable expectations teachers often face, we think that too often individuals allow their negative reactions to work circumstances override the otherwise positive aspects of their lives. As we said earlier, teachers have control over more than they realize. After all, we can always determine how we will react to situations. Changing our thought patterns is not easy, but it is a highly effective way to navigate the rough waters of our profession. As Lao Tzu once said, "Thoughts lead to actions, actions lead to habits, habits lead to character, and character changes destiny." So let's talk about changing thoughts.

SELIGMAN AND DELIBERATE OPTIMISM

Most of us are familiar with the term *learned helplessness*. It is a sociological expression generally used in education to refer to students who are not only reluctant learners, but who believe there is no way they can improve their circumstances. They tell us both with outward hostility and subtle withdrawal that they believe nothing they do makes any difference in the outcome of events. They think that bad things happen to them through misfortune and not because of logical consequences of their choices. Unfortunately, those students often grow up to be helpless, hopeless, bitter adults who are caught in a cycle of failure because their beliefs create actions that create circumstances that reinforce their original beliefs. In every sense, they have learned to be helpless.

In studying learned helplessness, Dr. Martin Seligman and Steven Maier (1967) conditioned a group of dogs by punishing them with electrical shocks. They put them in a box built with electrical coils on the bottom. They administered hurtful shocks to the dogs in a specific sequence. The dogs soon learned that if they performed a certain action, the shocks would stop. At the same time, they took another group of dogs and shocked them, too, but the shocks were arbitrarily administered, and nothing the second group of dogs did influenced the frequency or intensity of the shocks. Later the researchers put the first group of dogs in a double-sided shuttle box that had a shocking side and a nonshocking side. A low retaining barrier separated the two chambers. When the shock was applied to the first group of dogs, they quickly performed the trick they had learned for stopping the shocks. The trick no longer worked, so the dogs kept trying different strategies until each finally figured out all that was required to escape the shocks was to step over the barrier. Conversely, when the second group of dogs was tested (the dogs that had learned they had no control over the shocks), they simply lay down on top of the shocking coils and howled. They were inches away from relief, but they made no attempt to help themselves. Seligman surmised that he had taught the second group of dogs to be helpless.

Later Dr. Seligman decided to try to teach learned helplessness to humans. Thankfully, he did not use a shocking mechanism on people. Instead, he used loud sound to provide an irritant to members of the control group. He was surprised to find that unlike with dogs, he could not always condition people to be helpless. Many subjects refused to be helpless. Even though he attempted to condition them to believe they could not control the loud noise, several subjects refused to stop trying. They seemed to draw from an inner strength and would not accept that they were doomed to accepting the loud noise. From his observations, Seligman derived the term, *learned optimism*. Since those early experiments, he has continued to study and write about what factors are important for building resiliency and tenacity in people. When he was president of the American Psychiatric Association, he challenged his colleagues to quit focusing on why people have psychological problems and start working on how to help them live better lives. He believes that humans can learn to be optimistic by *unlearning* nonproductive thought patterns.

Seligman originated a plan he calls the "ABC Method." He believes that if you want to lead an optimistic life, you have to learn to argue with yourself in a non-negative way. In his book, *Learned Optimism: How to Change Your Mind and Your Life*, he describes how we can learn to lead ourselves into hope and action instead of despair.

The ABC Model

Adversity. The bad event or challenge you face.

Belief. Your default thinking or belief about the bad event or challenge. It's your explanation and interpretation of why things have gone wrong.

Consequences. The impact of your beliefs. It's what you feel and what you do as a result of your belief or interpretation of what happened. ■

SOURCE: Seligman (2006).

Our Five Principles of Deliberate Optimism parallel Seligman's ABC Model in that both ask participants to describe accurately the source of our angst, to examine more than one assumed motive for the cause, and to consider the long-term effect of our selected actions.

As an example, let's say your principal just informed you that next year instead of teaching the sixth-grade physical science classes you have taught for the past 7 years, she is reassigning you to teach eighth-grade earth science classes. You are appalled. You have spent years gathering resources and honing the lessons you use in teaching physical science. You assume you are being punished for some transgression, and you cannot believe you will no longer be teaching your favorite age group and preferred content. You just know that you will be stuck teaching eighth grade from now on, and you don't even like earth science. You are inconsolable about this change in your career; everyone knows how much you love teaching sixth grade, so this must be some kind of personal vendetta. Let's apply the ABC Model to this scenario.

> **Adversity.** You are being switched from teaching sixth-grade physical science to eighth-grade earth science.

> **Belief.** You believe this decision was made to punish you in some way and that you will be stuck with teaching your least favorite science for the rest of your time at that school. Teaching earth science will never be as much fun as teaching physical science.

> **Consequences.** You are hurt, angry, and fearful. You would like to get even with whomever made this decision. You know you are going to hate teaching earth science and you are not too crazy about teaching eighth graders. You decide you will let everyone know how unhappy you are and will stop doing all the many extras you do to help out around the school.

It is easy to get caught up in our protected *teaching terrains*. Teachers are some of the most territorial mammals on this planet. How many of us write our names on every piece of furniture, equipment, material, and piece of flotsam in our proximity? Many of us like to take ownership of a particular subject area, seat in the lounge, or even our favorite place to park. Defaulting to the *They* versus *Us* mentality is sometimes an automatic reaction when we perceive that someone is trying to take something that is ours. But does it help us long term to feel victimized and offended?

Personalizing adversity only makes it worse as does viewing obstacles as *permanent* and *pervasive*. Perhaps we need to do a better job of trying to argue ourselves out of these perceptions.

The ABCD Model

DISPUTATION

Seligman refers to arguing with our thoughts as *disputation*. It's a key practice for building optimism. It works by countering our negative thoughts with deliberation and reflection. To dispute our negative thoughts, we can practice with his ABCD method.

First we must identify the adversity, our beliefs, and the likely consequences of those beliefs. Next, we must dispute our beliefs and be aware of how different perceptions change the consequences. For example, if we originally explained our adversity with beliefs that are **permanent, personal**, and **pervasive**, we feel paralyzed and defeated. Alternately, if we explain our beliefs as **temporary, external**, and **specific**, we create hope, which leads to action.

FOUR WAYS TO IMPROVE YOUR DISPUTATION

According to Seligman, there are four ways you can dispute your beliefs more effectively:

> **Evidence**. Ask yourself, "What's the evidence you have for and against the belief?" *(My principal isn't known for making arbitrary decisions. I know that she respects me as a teacher. There have been concerns about the lack of active learning in eighth grade. Perhaps I am being moved there to be a model for the other eighth-grade teachers.)*

> **Alternatives**. Ask yourself, "Is there another way to look at the adversity?" *(If I am totally honest with myself, I've grown a little complacent about my sixth-grade class. I could almost teach physical science in my sleep. Moving to a new area is probably going to help me stay challenged, and I have always performed better when I'm challenged.)*

Implications. Ask yourself, "What's the impact?" Assuming that your negative explanation is right, check whether you are making mountains out of molehills. *(I'm probably not going to like teaching eighth grade as much as I do sixth grade, but I guess at least I will still be teaching middle school science. My first love is middle school, and my second love is science, so this really isn't the end of the world.)*

Usefulness. Ask yourself, "Is this a good time for me to be thinking about this problem?" If now is not the time, then either do something physically distracting, schedule another time to with yourself to think things over, or write the negative thoughts down and deal with them when you're ready. *("This assignment change could not have come at a worse time. I have got to have knee surgery in a couple of weeks, I'm trying to study for finals in my graduate courses, and I've got to put my car in the shop this Friday. This is not the best time for me to be thinking about all the changes I will have to make next year. I think I'll put those thoughts on hold for a few weeks until the rest of my life settles down a bit.")* Being able to compartmentalize our worries and address them at appropriate times is a good first step toward handling difficulty with optimism.

Disputing your negative thoughts might help you change your perception and the consequences of your altered perception as follows:

Adversity. You are being switched from teaching sixth-grade physical science to eighth-grade earth science.

Belief. You have no idea why you are being switched, but you feel confident it has nothing to do with you personally. You have really enjoyed teaching sixth-grade physical science, but you are a good teacher, and you believe you can learn to do an effective job teaching earth science, too. You have no idea how long this assignment will last, so if you don't like teaching eighth-grade science, you will take steps to get moved back to teaching sixth-grade science.

Consequences. You are curious about why this decision was made and are anxious to speak with your administrator about why you are being moved. You know that you are a team player and will try to accommodate whatever works best for all concerned. You hope you'll learn to like teaching eighth-grade earth science as much as you do sixth-grade physical science. You are already thinking of some resources you can tap to help you get started.

The ABCDE Model

Seligman concludes his model with an *E* for *energization*. He notes that when we dispute our negative thinking and replace it with reasoning that is reflective and grounded in beliefs about our best selves, we change defeat and depression into hope and energy. He calls this step *energization*. He writes about a familiar teaching situation:

Adversity. I haven't been able to break through the apathy that some of my students feel toward learning.

Belief. Why can't I reach these kids? If I were more dynamic or more creative or more intelligent, I would be able to excite them about learning. If I can't reach the kids who need the most help, then I am not doing my job. I must not be cut out for teaching.

Consequence. I don't feel like being creative. I have little energy and I feel depressed and dejected.

Disputation. It doesn't make sense to base my worth as a teacher on a small percentage of my students. The truth is, I do excite the majority of my students, and I spend a great deal of time planning lessons that are creative and allow the students as much individualization as possible. At the end of the term, when I have a little more time, I can organize a meeting with other teachers in the school who face this same problem. Maybe as a group we will be able to come up with some ideas that will help us reach the apathetic students.

Energization. I feel better about the work I do as a teacher and hopeful that new ideas can be generated through a discussion with other teachers. (Seligman, 2006, p. 270)

You may be thinking, "Well, it's easy to list all those steps, but can we really control our thoughts that way?" We believe we can all control our thoughts. It's not always an easy or even a simple process, but with practice, it can become a habit. We can start reclaiming our joy in teaching by becoming aware of the power we already have.

SELF-DETERMINATION

As experienced teachers, we have to admit that each of us has spent some time in the *ain't it awful* place. You know the situation; a bunch of educators gather to collectively bemoan the obstacles that keep us from doing a great job as teachers. It generally starts with someone shaking his or her head and saying things like, "Well, the principal just informed me that I have to cover all of my bulletin boards during standardized test week. There's not one thing on those boards that will influence a student's answers, but he says just it's a rule that every teacher will cover all informational material on bulletin boards and classroom walls. That is such a waste of time! There is no reason to burden us with such a stupid mandate." The surrounding group members shake their heads in misery as they do the familiar *ain't it awful* routine. No one offers a possible explanation, a plan, or a solution to the challenge. Participants simply hang their heads and say, "Look what *They* are doing to *Us* now. Ain't it *awful?*"

Us and *They* are two powerful words that can diminish the optimism within a school. For example, a teacher sends a student to the office and is unhappy about the results. She tells her coworkers, "I sent Draco to the office, and *They* did nothing! I guess the *powers that be* don't care one bit about *Us* and what *We* are having to put up with in our classrooms." Using the term *They* in this context is divisive and pits the teachers against those in administration. Laying blame without even trying to find out the facts or seeing the perspective of the other person contributes to an erosion of trust and cooperation among the adults at school. We teachers need to focus more on what we can control rather than trying to micromanage what we perceive others should be doing.

Another problem with the "Look what *They* are doing to *Us*" mentality is that it robs us of power. It suggests that we are helpless against forces that at best do not care about us and at worst are out to get us. Edward Deci and Richard Ryan, University of Rochester, have spent years investigating the general theory of motivation. Their work has influenced over three decades of research on the influence of certain factors supporting the individual's natural or intrinsic tendencies to behave in effective and productive ways (see Deci & Ryan, 2000; Ryan & Deci, 2000). They and others conclude that increasing an individual's autonomy, competency, and relatedness has a positive effect on his or her *self-determination* (SDT). And it is self-determination that regulates internalizing and maintaining positive behaviors.

AUTONOMY

One of the greatest contributors to a teachers' optimism is the extent to which they feel they control their own destiny. We hear from teachers about their increasing feelings of helplessness. Top-down decisions are affecting their freedom to choose the way they teach, the pace at which they teach, and their individuality as educators. Along with large-scale testing comes large-scale prep and remediation programs (often from the same companies, hmmmm), which prescribe the exact methods and allocated time for instruction. Some of their materials go so far as to script the curriculum in an effort to make their lessons *teacher proof.* Perhaps a beginning teacher would welcome a few scripted lessons to practice his or her new skills for a short while, but for the most part, teachers feel insulted by admonitions to "stick to the script" rather than to creatively address the learning goals with their best practices and based on their knowledge of the students in their classrooms.

> Sacrificing your personal life to the classroom may seem like a sign of dedication, but is more likely to lead to burnout and bad attitude. We all need time to go home, turn the teaching dial down, and go back to being a person with a first name.
>
> —Roxanna Elden, author of *See Me After Class*

After telling teachers for decades to look for teachable moments and to do everything we can to personalize lessons to their students' interests, there is now a push to standardize most every aspect of the classroom experience. Stanford University Education Professor Nel Noddings (2014) writes, "Freedom to plan and teach creatively is conducive to both higher morale and a deeper sense of responsibility" (p. 18).

One of the things that attracts educators to the profession is the fundamental understanding that we will be able to make decisions about what goes on in our classrooms. Whether we have long dreamed of replicating our own happy classroom experiences or whether we want to try something entirely different from what we perceived as ineffective when we were in school, we did not aspire to become automatons who merely recite programmed directions and administer summative tests. We believe that teachers should be trusted to communicate essential ideas and to connect with our students in ways we deem most effective. If and when students are not mastering the knowledge and skills they need or are alienated by a teacher's attitude, corrective action can be taken through peer and/or administrative intervention. We want to feel trusted.

COMPETENCE

One's optimism is largely determined by the degree to which a person feels able to influence desired outcomes. The more competent individuals feel, the more likely they are to enjoy their job. In many ways, the opposite of learned helplessness is what Albert Bandura (1997) calls *self-efficacy*.

> *Self–belief does not necessarily ensure success, but self–disbelief assuredly spawns failure.*
>
> —Bandura (1997, p. 77)

Bandura refers to competence and self-belief as *self-efficacy*. Perceived self-efficacy refers to one's impression of what one is capable of doing. Self-efficacy comes from

There is an old story about a veteran maintenance person who was transferred to a new school. The principal proudly showed him around the campus instructing him on how he wanted it maintained. In the teacher workroom, the principal made a show of unlocking a large storeroom filled with paper, pencils, and all kinds of supplies and materials a teacher might need to use in her classroom. The principal told the custodian he would be in charge of restocking and maintaining the closet, but that he was to keep it locked at all other times. "We have to keep it secure because we can't trust our teachers with these school supplies."

The old custodian shook his head and asked quietly, "But you trust them with the kids?"

> *In our school we have regularly scheduled meetings on Tuesday afternoons. Usually we meet with our departments, but once a month we have committee meetings for our standing committees (like hospitality, grounds and safety, curriculum, school climate, parental involvement, public relations, etc.). Other than the committee chairs and cochairs faculty members are free to choose which committee meeting they want to attend. Because we get to select where we will go, we are more willing to participate in schoolwide committees.*
>
> —Thomas Cuttler, high school math department chair

a variety of sources, such as personal accomplishments and failures, watching others who are similar to oneself, and verbal persuasion from valued others. Bandura is quick to point out that verbal persuasion may temporarily convince us that we should try or should avoid some tasks, but in the final analysis, it is our direct or vicarious experience with success or failure that will most strongly influence our self-efficacy. For example, a beginning of the year opening motivational conclave may temporarily inspire teachers, but their enthusiasm will be short-lived if their job requirements are completely beyond their ability or their perceived beliefs that they can actually do well.

Bandura explains how important it is to focus on the two things over which each of us always has control—**our choices** and **our efforts**. He maintains that those two concepts are the keys to earned success. When we believe that through our efforts we can get markedly better at anything we deliberately practice and that our circumstances are largely determined by the choices we make, we become acutely aware of the amount of power we have over our destiny.

People with high-perceived self-efficacy try more, accomplish more, and persist longer at a task than people with low-perceived self-efficacy. Bandura (1986) speculates that this is because people with high-perceived self-efficacy tend to feel they have more control over their environment and, therefore, experience less uncertainty.

So how do we go about increasing our self-efficacy? Part of the answer lies in the research done by attribution theorists. In examining why people think they either were or were not successful in achieving their goals, researchers found that all of the rationales and explanations people offered basically fell into four categories. Subjects believed their success or lack of it was mainly dependent one of these four things:

- The difficulty of the task
- The innate ability or talent of the participant
- The luck or fate involved
- The effort extended

Look again at these factors. One of them is different from the others in an important way. Do you see which one? Three of these have to do with external forces, things over which individuals have no control. People cannot control the difficulty of their life challenges. They did not get to pick which or how much natural talent and ability they were born with. And despite what compulsive gamblers believe, no one controls luck. The only one among the four factors over which a person has direct influence is **effort**. It is both disconcerting and empowering to realize that most of our present situations are shaped by the choices we made and the amount of deliberate effort we were willing to put forth. People with a high degree of self-efficacy have developed the ability required to implement Seligman's ABCDE Model. They are less likely to personalize adversity or see it as permanent or pervasive. Self–efficacy helps us to view challenges as temporary and surmountable; it helps us focus on action rather than on blame.

> *People not only gain understanding through reflection, they evaluate and alter their own thinking.*
>
> —Bandura (1986, p. 21)

RELATEDNESS

We will discuss the role of relatedness to students in Chapter 5, but here we would like to talk about individual teachers relating their current work to a larger picture. Self-efficacy is an essential part of optimism, and it applies not only to individuals, but also to organizations. Bandura (2009) believes that *organizational efficacy* is much like individual efficacy, but with more influence from outside forces. In organizations, people generally have to rely on each other, at least to some extent, to accomplish their tasks.

In the most successful schools we have worked in and visited, we have found these collective attributes—a common vision, a shared values system, effective communication among all personnel, demonstrated mutual respect, and a sense of appropriate playfulness. Along with these attributes, great schools have trust within the building and the capacity to hold each other accountable.

> *We try to pretend we are at IBM— we treat everyone as a professional and we celebrate when we can. The material things are nice, but I have a motto that I try to live by each day: My job is to make the teacher's job easier, better, so they can teach students.*
>
> —Tony Pallija, principal (as quoted in "How to Keep Good Teachers Motivated," n.d.)

Schools with those characteristics in place generally have the efficacy required to face adversity (even budget cuts, high *sweepstakes* testing, and large scale curriculum shifts) with perseverance and resilience.

In speaking about developing and instilling resilience in others, author/poet Maya Angelou says:

I'm not sure if resilience is ever achieved alone. Experience allows us to learn from example. But if we have someone who loves us—I don't mean who indulges us, but who loves us enough to be on our side—then it's easier to grow resilience, to grow belief in self, to grow self-esteem. And it's self-esteem that allows a person to stand up. (Azzam, 2013, p. 10)

Ms. Angelou is primarily talking about building resiliency in children through their families, but we think her words are also true for a school community. School communities need to function as family units, and we the teachers, too, need to stand by each other, encourage each other, and demand the best of each other. We believe that all the adults at school should stand together. (Even though we are outnumbered by the kids, at least standing together gives us a fighting chance.)

We recommend that schools purposefully work on their organizational efficacy. We often look outside of schools to find what other organizations do to help employees feel related as well as competent. We like the core values of the shoe corporation, Zappos Company. Imagine the possibilities of a school that practiced their principles:

The Zappos Company Core Values

1. Deliver the WOW Through Service

2. Embrace and Drive Change

3. Create Fun and a Little Weirdness

4. Be Adventurous, Creative, and Open-Minded

5. Pursue Growth and Learning

6. Build Open and Honest Relationships With Communication

7. Build a Positive Team and Family Spirit

8. Do More With Less

9. Be Passionate and Be Determined

10. Be Humble ■

SOURCE: Zappos Company (n.d.).

The Zappos Company Philosophy

We value passion, determination, perseverance, and the sense of urgency.

We are inspired because we believe in what we are doing and where we are going. We don't take "no" or "that'll never work" for an answer because if we had, then Zappos would have never started in the first place.

Passion and determination are contagious. We believe in having a positive and optimistic (but realistic) attitude about everything we do because we realize that this inspires others to have the same attitude.

There is excitement in knowing that everyone you work with has a tremendous impact on a larger dream and vision, and you can see that impact day in and day out. ∎

SOURCE: Zappos Company (n.d.).

Basically, what we are saying is that each of us has the power over our choices and our efforts. We can work to change our thoughts, and we can help those around us learn to be positive and optimistic. Optimism is a learned thought pattern that is not inherent, is not simple, and is not easy. But optimism is achievable, and it is important for us as teachers to consciously develop our autonomy, our competence, and our relatedness.

Action Steps for Teachers

DISCUSSION QUESTIONS AND ACTIVITIES

1. How do you define optimism? On a scale of 1–10 (with 1 being Eeyore and 10 being Pollyanna), where would you put yourself as an optimist? Why? Take one or more of the happiness and optimism tests listed in the Appendix, page 141. Do you agree with your results? Why or why not?

2. Do you agree with the authors that people learn to be helpless? Do you think helplessness can be *unlearned*? Give examples to support your beliefs.

3. Think of a recent issue that was upsetting to you as a teacher. Apply Seligman's ABCDE Model to what happened. Discuss how this model could be helpful to you or to other teachers.

4. Describe the amount of autonomy you feel you have in your classroom. How does that affect how you do your job? What could you do to increase your autonomy?

5. How willing are you to accept responsibility for your circumstances? Give one or two examples of when you were able to attribute your success or failure to something over which you had direct control. How did that affect your next step?

6. What is the general quality of faculty relationships on your campus? Do you feel valued and appreciated by your colleagues? Why or why not?

7. Without reviewing what has been written in the past, write a set of core values and a philosophy you would like to have for your class, your team, or your school.

8. Starting now, what are some steps you could take to become a more optimistic educator? What is preventing you from doing that?

9. If you were Ruler of Education within your school for a year, what changes would you make to help with school morale?

10. As a group, list 10 things that cost little or nothing that could be put into place at your school right now that would positively impact teacher morale. Designate two or three group members to share these with your school leaders.

11. Visit the ProTeacher social network (www.proteacher.net) frequently and offer your own contributions when you can.

Action Steps for School Leaders

1. If your staff wants to learn more about how to combat learned helplessness in students and the power of mindsets on learning, you and your staff can to do a book study on Debbie Silver's bestselling book, *Fall Down 7 Times, Get Up 8: Teaching Kids to Succeed* (2013a, Corwin).

2. Either you or your counselor can administer Seligman's Optimism Test and allow staff members to discuss their results. (See www.stanford.edu/class/msande271/onlinetools/LearnedOpt.html.)

3. With your staff, brainstorm an ABCDE Model of dealing with a current school issue.

4. Review the Zappos Company Core Values. Ask teachers to compare and contrast Zappos core values with those of your school. Ask small groups to write a completely new school philosophy that reflects the group's core beliefs and put it on poster paper or PowerPoint slide to share with the whole group.

5. In the lounge or other central location, put up a Morale Graffti Board. Encourage staff members to write or draw ideas for improving morale among the adults at school.

6. Adopt a new teacher program. New teachers have so many expenses and costs. Ask local businesses to donate meal cards, classroom supplies, classroom plants and decorations, and other items helpful to newcomers just starting out.

7. Write occasional notes to staff members telling them what you value in them and thanking them for how they contribute to the positive morale at your school.

8. Have random drawings throughout the year for staff members that include things like gift cards, weekend getaways, or a half-day sub.

9. If you have young staff members, be mindful of the demands of new parenthood. As much as possible, provide new parents with temporary relief from evening duties, time and a private place for nursing mothers to pump, and occasional late arrival and early departure privileges, if needed. Find someone to fill in for them or volunteer to cover the class yourself.

10. For staff members who are caretakers for aging parents or sick family members, offer occasional late arrival and early departure privileges as well as occasional relief from after school and evening duties. Just knowing that you are aware and supportive goes a long way.

11. Make sure that all staff members have the supplies they need to do their jobs. Stock storerooms (or better yet, individual classrooms) with plenty of tissues, hand sanitizer, paper, cleaning solution, paper towels, bandages, markers, pens, pencils, and whatever teachers need. Don't make them justify every request. If a teacher needs materials to do his or her job, move mountains to get what he or she needs.

CHAPTER 3

"But We Have This ONE Teacher Who Keeps Ruining Things for Everyone!"

I could be more of a people person if everybody else didn't suck so much!

—Rhodeena Culsmucker

Have you ever felt that it would be easier to be optimistic if you could just get rid of one or two (or 10 or 20) of your colleagues? One of the authors of this book takes on a comedy persona, a curmudgeon schoolteacher named Rhodeena Culsmucker, who is the classic pessimist. She sees only the negative in her administrators, her students, and her colleagues. A sharp decrease in the joy factor is felt the moment she walks into a gathering. She is cynical, critical, mean-spirited, and of course, quite verbal. She is the antithesis of what we want and need from our colleagues. And yet every time our author portrays her in a comedy skit, teachers immediately say, "Oh my gosh, I work with a guy (or gal) just like that!"

In truth, the character, Rhodeena Culsmucker, speaks to every teacher because she is the epitome of our very worst selves. We laugh at her because her growling and complaining echo our lowest thoughts and even things we have said in our own flawed moments. She's funny because she's not a real teacher. Really negative strident colleagues are vexations to the soul. They are not funny, and they can be quite damaging not only to those around them but also to an entire school environment.

We are often asked what to do about a colleague who is constantly downbeat and disapproving. People are inquiring about a teacher who refuses to be a team player and subverts colleagues who are trying to make things better. Let's review the Principles of Deliberate Optimism:

Five Principles of Deliberate Optimism

1. Before acting or reacting, **gather as much information** from as many varied sources as possible.

2. **Determine what is beyond your control** and strategize how to minimize its impact on your life.

3. **Establish what you can control** and seek tools and strategies to help you maximize your power.

4. Actively **DO something positive** toward your goal.

5. **Take ownership** of your plan and acknowledge responsibility for your choices. ∎

Principle number one suggests that before making a judgment about anything, we gather as much information from as many varied sources as possible. We think there are three major areas that need to be addressed when informing ourselves about why people act the way they do—mind (learning) style, extrovert or introvert tendencies, and generational differences. Developing a better understanding of behavior in ourselves and in others is our goal for Chapter 3.

GATHER AS MUCH INFORMATION AS YOU CAN

In our experience, we have found that off-putting behavior is sometimes most notable when groups are trying to implement change. Rhodeena Culsmucker says, "I don't mind change as long as I don't have to do anything differently." Occasionally, this seems to be the attitude of some of our peers. But is that really what they are saying? If we look a little deeper, could it be that they are basically trying to accommodate new policies and assimilate new procedures in a way that best suits their inherent styles? Perhaps they are not trying so much to "rain on our parades" as to deal with challenges in the best way they know how.

LEARNING STYLES

Dr. Anthony Gregorc (1984), author of the *Mind Styles Model,* is a phenomenology researcher and author who studies the different ways people best acquire and assimilate new information. His belief is that people inherently differ in the manner they approach problem solving and the ways they make sense of their environments. He writes, "It appears that dispositions for interacting with the world in specific ways are inborn" (p. 52). His longstanding investigation into learning styles has led to some interesting thoughts. Perhaps the behavior that outsiders perceive as antisocial, fussy, compulsive, flighty, frivolous, and the like are actually just compensatory ways that certain people use to make sense of their worlds. Maybe if we better understood the needs of people with different learning styles, we could start to see that they are not actually trying to go against us or to be difficult, but rather that they are doing what comes naturally to them when coping with life.

Dr. Gregorc believes the mind works on a **perceptual** level and on an **ordering** level. Perceptual qualities generally lean toward concrete or abstract.

> *When my late husband passed away as a result of colon cancer, and I took his body home to be buried, I was gone for a week. I had used up all of my sick days during his illness and expenses were tight. My peers made a schedule of my classes and volunteered to teach during their prep periods so that I would not have to pay a sub, and my students wouldn't suffer in my absence. They took over and made sure my students had solid learning experiences while I was away. My gratitude to them is beyond measure. I can't imagine teaching in a school where staff members do not support one another.*
>
> —Joyce Patton, science teacher, Shreveport, LA

Concrete. This quality enables you to register information directly through your five senses: sight, smell, touch, taste, and hearing. When you are using your concrete ability, you are dealing with the obvious, the "here and now." You are not looking for hidden meanings, or making relationships between ideas or concepts. **"It is what it is."**

Abstract. This quality allows you to visualize, to conceive ideas, to understand or believe that which you cannot actually see. When you are using your abstract quality, you are using your intuition, your imagination, and you are looking beyond "what is" to the more subtle implications. **"It is not always what it seems."**

He thinks that an individual's ordering ability normally manifests itself as sequential or random.

Sequential. Allows your mind to organize information in a **linear,** step-by-step manner. When using your sequential ability, you are following a logical train of thought, a traditional approach to dealing with information. You may also prefer to have a plan and to follow it, rather than relying on impulse.

Random. Lets your mind organize information by **chunks,** and in no particular order. When you are using your random ability, you may often be able to skip steps in a procedure and still produce the desired result. You may even start in the middle, or at the end, and work backward. You may also prefer your life to be more impulsive, or spur of the moment, than planned. (Gregorc, n.d.)

Gregorc (1982) believes that even though both ordering abilities are present in individuals, people are generally more comfortable using one than the other. His classifications are determined by the strongest perceptive abilities paired with the compelling ordering abilities, and they are as follows:

1. Concrete Sequential (CS)

2. Abstract Random (AR)

3. Abstract Sequential (AS)

4. Concrete Random (CR)

While no one is totally one style, most people default to one of these categories because of their basic inclinations. Below are descriptions of people in each of the groups. See if you can find yourself, and also try to identify some behaviors in others that are typical for their learning styles.

Concrete Sequential (CS)

The CS is a lover of neatness, order, and detail. She wants specific directions and does not like to be distracted when learning. Her preference is to do one activity at a time. She likes direct instruction with hands-on practice. Her approach to change is slow and incremental. She likes to be in control of most situations, and she does not like surprises. She avoids unpredictable people and circumstances.

The CS is factual, organized, dependable, and punctual. Most CS's believe that you are actually a little late if you show up right on time. They are hardworking, consistent, and accurate. They are great at following directions and meeting deadlines. They are usually conservative and always consistent.

Does this sound like you or someone you know? Depending on your own style, you may or may not be able to relate to this person because she has a hard time working in groups. It's difficult for her to delegate tasks because others "won't do it right." Dealing with abstract ideas or requests to "use your imagination" is also not easy for her. She is uncomfortable in unorganized environments, and she prefers to make changes in a limited, methodical, supported manner.

If this is not your style, you may see her as a bit of a "fussbudget" who is something of a control freak. You may resent her wanting to do things in a particular order and insisting that the rest of you follow all the rules. You may feel like she doesn't ever want to change so you give up on her. However, using the methodology Seligman talks about in Chapter 2, what if you reframed your thinking by changing your beliefs about this person? Instead of labeling her a nitpicking perfectionist out to ruin every new idea, what if you acknowledge she really just needs to have a logically sequenced, well-structured challenge in order to feel comfortable?

Perhaps it would be helpful to take the extra effort to make sure when you present your ideas to this colleague that you focus on step-by-step instructions and real-life examples. Taking the time to see the valuable organizational skills this person has to offer will help you not only view her in a more favorable light, but will also help her feel more valued and probably more cooperative. (Also this person usually makes a great choice as team leader.)

Abstract Random (AR)

Is there someone with whom you work that wakes up in a new world every day? Does this person constantly lose his train of thought, switch subjects with no warning, and bounce around like Tigger in *Winnie the Pooh*? It sounds as though we are describing someone with attention deficit/hyperactivity disorder (ADHD), but in reality, there is a learning style called Abstract Random, which has characteristics very similar to some of those identified with the ADHD syndrome.

AR's are spontaneous, flexible, and quick to "jump on the bandwagon" as long as they believe in the idea. This individual is sensitive, compassionate, perceptive, and sentimental. He pays attention to human detail. This is the colleague who notices if you've lost weight, if you've done something different with your hair, or if you are worried about something outside of school. He is usually a people pleaser who loves to bring together all sorts of folks for discussions, activities, or just hanging out. He is lively, colorful, and full of energy.

On the other hand, the AR has a great deal of trouble dealing with people who are bossy, negative, or unfriendly. He prefers to multitask rather than work on one thing at a time. He has difficulty following rules and restrictions, and he has trouble accepting even positive criticism.

AR's are generally poor time managers, and they sometimes fail to finish projects they start. People not of this ilk sometimes see them as flakey, outlandish, or just plain weird. They doubt the AR's substance and don't trust him with anything important. AR's prefer to just "jump right in" and deal with the consequences later. In meetings, they enjoy talking off topic and dealing with feelings rather than facts.

If you are not an AR, you may be reticent to deal with one. However, if you look at this person under a different lens, maybe you can see that he does have substance, but he sometimes doesn't show it because he's always off on the next tangent when you are still finalizing the steps in the previous one (which, by the way, is one he started and lost interest in). With the understanding that AR's are extremely sensitive and in tune with others, maybe you could simply say to him, "Robin, can you slow down a bit? I love that you always have new ideas, but we really need you to help finish this project first. You are quite the cheerleader, and we really could use your enthusiasm to complete this part before we go on."

Rather than dismiss the AR as someone you can't count on, it's probably more productive to focus on his ability to listen to others and to energize others' efforts. You eventually might be able to help him recognize how strongly his emotions affect his concentration.

Abstract Sequential (AS)

You would think that with four learning styles you could expect to find about 25 percent of educators in each category. You would be wrong. It has been our experience that generally less than 10 percent of faculties and staff are Abstract Sequentials. AS's are found in abundance at the university level, but not so much in K–12 settings. The reason there are few of them in traditional schools is evident when you examine who they are. AS's thrive on research and do not like being hurried to make a decision. They like to have the time to thoroughly explore a topic before moving on. They prefer to direct their own learning and to work alone. They are highly skeptical and dislike distractions.

The AS at your school may be a person who demands references for everything you state. She wants to know the credentials of the person or persons behind the idea you are proposing and has little patience with "small talk" or sentimental rhetoric. It's not that she is unwilling to change, but you are never going to win her over with a moving story, well-timed music, or a group hug. She needs to see facts and figures. She is a voracious reader, but she often fails to pick up on social cues. (She might remind you of Sheldon on *The Big Bang Theory*.)

AS's have great difficulty working with people who have differing opinions from theirs. If left unchecked, they can monopolize the conversation with little awareness of the feelings of others. Their motto is "knowledge is power." Behind her back, you may call her "Ms. Know-It-All" or something less kind. You may feel that she doesn't value you or your feelings so you avoid her when you can.

The problem with dismissing the AS is that you are missing an opportunity to relate to someone who is excellent at applying logic in solving or finding solutions to problems. Because of all she reads, she probably has a wealth of knowledge she could share with you and your colleagues. Her analysis of the finer points of issues and proposals can provide invaluable information when trying to reach a decision. This is the person who not only enjoys doing the research, but also is able to tease out the key points and significant details.

So rather than feeling defensive and oppressed by this colleague, why not consider that hurting your feelings is not her intent? Like all of us, she has her own peculiarities that are born from her need to deal with the world in a way that makes her comfortable. When she corrects you or questions you about your thinking, just understand that she probably doesn't mean it as an attack. She really wants to know how you came to your conclusion. However, be aware that she is more persuaded by facts than by emotion, and she has little regard for hearsay or gossip.

Concrete Random (CR)

The CR has the philosophy, "If it ain't broke, break it!" Like Concrete Sequentials, they are based in reality, but because of their random nature, they generally like change just because they are ready for something different. Sometimes they are the instigators of change. This person is inquisitive and independent. He does not read directions, but instead, he solves everything with a trial-and-error approach. He gets the gist of ideas quickly and demonstrates the uncanny ability to make intuitive leaps when exploring unstructured problem-solving experiences. He is usually self-motivated and not interested in details.

The CR on your staff is often a technology specialist, a science teacher, or someone in an innovative discipline. He has an experimental attitude about everything, and he sometimes goes off on his own leaving his colleagues behind. CR's have a strong need to do things in their own way. They do not like formal reports, keeping detailed records, routines, or redoing anything once it is done. Sometimes CR's are seen as mavericks who are too independent and poor team players, but that isn't necessarily true.

CR's have a tremendous capacity for accepting many different kinds of people as well as offering unique ways of doing things. They contribute unusual and creative ideas, and they are able to visualize the future. Rather than trying to "rein them in," you can support their investigational approach to life and get them to help you explore your own preconceived barriers.

Because they are usually risk takers, CR's can benefit from working with sequentials who are usually more able to anticipate possible pitfalls and trouble spots as well as adhere to deadlines. Sometimes others are put off by a perceived impatience in a CR, but upon closer examination, you may find that they are just colleagues who want to be doing rather than talking. These adventurous individuals can spark creativity in others with their intuitive, innovative thinking. As with the other three learning styles, CR's have their challenges as well as their positive qualities.

One major step toward accepting others is realizing that every style of being has its tradeoffs. Strength in one area often is counterbalanced by a weakness in another. Taking the time and patience to understand the true nature of a colleague's idiosyncrasies can lead to a huge payoff in building a connection with that person. Changing your beliefs about why they make some of the choices they do can change the consequences of your feelings about them. Reclaiming your joy for teaching starts with rebuilding your relationships with those who share the work you do.

We recommend that the adults at school take **The Gregorc Style Delineator** (or some other instrument that explores basic style approaches) together and discuss the implications of their results. Generally, individuals are delighted to be able to "put a finger on" why some people act the way they do. We find it rewarding when interacting adults start to realize that many things that "get on their last nerve" (with both adults and students) are actually just coping mechanisms of the offending party intrinsic to his particular learning style. It is much easier to tolerate the habitual lateness of a colleague when we realize he is random and probably has no idea what time it is rather than attributing it to some kind of passive-aggressive act directed toward us. Just changing the labels from "He's so anal retentive" to "Well, that's his concrete sequential nature" is a positive step toward building community. The Gregorc Style Delineator is available for purchase online (http://gregorc.com/instrume.html).

Gregorc's Mind Styles Model can certainly provide insight into human behavior. His theory is not the only one out there, nor is it universally accepted. Whatever learning style, learning preference, multiple intelligence, or personality theory you subscribe to, we think it's important to gather information and think deeply about the way humans act and interact. After all, dealing with humans (both big and small) is our primary job. For more resources, see the Appendix, "Websites for Getting to Know Ourselves and Each Other," page 142.

EXTROVERTS AND INTROVERTS

There are some people who really seem to dislike just about everyone. Even when you try to include them in your group, they resist. They procrastinate about getting involved in team-building activities, they decline invitations to special faculty events, and sometimes they seem to prefer eating alone in their rooms rather than joining others in the lounge or lunchroom. It would be easy to label them as aloof, unfriendly, cold, detached, or even unapproachable. We have heard teachers say about such a person, "Well, I guess she just thinks she's too good to hang out with the rest of us. Maybe we're not worthy of her attention." Those kinds of comments are generally made by someone who defines herself or himself by the friends she or he has and has little understanding of people who draw strength from being alone.

> I work well with others, as long as they stay out of my personal space, don't make any noise, and don't expect me to communicate with them in any way.
>
> —Rhodeena Culsmucker

When you study personality theory, you inevitably come across the terms *introvert* and *extrovert*. Two of the authors of this book are generally classified as extroverts for most situations. As extrovert teachers, we tried to *fix* our introverted students so they could enjoy a more robust, fulfilled lifestyle. When dealing with colleagues, we felt sorry for the introverts and jumped in quickly to fill the gaps when they didn't speak, commit, or participate. On reflection, we see that we did not do them any favors.

Most of us were taught that introverts are simply people who are shy. Extroverts, on the other hand, are outspoken, confident, and filled with leadership potential. Recently, much has been written on the subject of introversion and how it has been misinterpreted. Behavior experts contend that introversion itself is not shyness. According to Bainbridge (2014),

> Shyness has an element of apprehension, nervousness, and anxiety, and while an introvert may be also shy, introversion itself is not shyness. Basically, an introvert is a person who is energized by being alone and whose energy is drained by being around other people.

In her book, *Quiet: The Power of Introverts in a World That Won't Stop Talking* (2012), journalist/researcher Susan Cain points out that an introvert might identify with at least some of the following attributes: thoughtful, serious, inner-directed, calm, sensitive, unassuming, shy, and solitude seeking. Conversely, an extrovert might identify with some of these attributes: gregarious, excitable, active, risk-taking, light-hearted, and thick-skinned. While not comprehensive, this list serves as a starting point to understanding the differences between the two categories.

> *The funny thing about introverts is once they feel comfortable with you, they can be the funniest, most enjoyable people to be around. It's like a secret they feel comfortable sharing with you. Except the secret is their personality.*
>
> —Anonymous

Cain states that nearly one third of the people we know are introverts. In an era that values outgoing, charismatic people who demonstrate confidence, a kind of *extrovert ideal* has marginalized that third, who sometimes are our deepest, most thoughtful thinkers. Perhaps in trying to understand our quieter colleagues, we need to rethink how we sometimes talk over them, ignore them, and otherwise dismiss them as not as important as their more forceful peers.

One of the key informational pieces we need to know about the people with whom we work (both our colleagues and our students) is whether they are predominantly introverts or extroverts. Most of us are knowledgeable about dealing with extroverts, but could an intentional focus on the introverts in our lives help us better understand how to interact with them? Dan Rockwell, author of the blog, *Leadership Freak* (2013) warns against underestimating quiet people. He cautions that it is dangerous to assume that silence is consent and urges colleagues to give quiet people a chance to collect their thoughts before they have to make a commitment or frame an answer. In his blog, *10 Ways to "Deal With" Quiet People*, Rockwell advises:

1. Honor their strengths. Never say, "Oh, they're quiet," like it's a disease.

2. Respect their ability to commit. When they're in, they're in.

3. Give them prep time. Don't spring things on them.

4. Don't assume silence is disagreement or consent. Just don't assume.

5. Enjoy silence. Give them space by closing your mouth.

6. Ask questions, after you've given them think-time.

7. Invite feedback one-on-one rather than in groups.

8. Walk with them after meetings and ask, "What's going through your mind?" The walking part is important.

9. Create quiet environments. Quiet people often enjoy quiet places.

10. Let them work alone. Stop demanding group work.

SOURCE: Rockwell (2013).

If you are not an introvert, it is important to familiarize yourself with their characteristics and predilections. Most of them enjoy being with a few trusted associates occasionally, but they thrive on *downtime* when they can spend moments alone rejuvenating themselves. If you are an introvert, you need to understand that extroverts like to *think out loud,* and try not to judge them harshly because of their excessive chatter. Extroverts are as energized by being around others as you are from spending time alone. Knowing all we can about one another's preferences is the first step toward building a healthy communication among educators.

GENERATIONAL DIFFERENCES

Another piece of information we think is relevant to guiding our thinking about others is the phenomena of generational differences. For the first time in our history, we have three and sometimes even four different generations working in the same school. Social psychologists and other researchers point out that each generation comes with its own distinct attitudes, expectations, and habits with regard to work. At times, we may find ourselves at cross-purposes merely because of when we were born.

> I think all this newfangled technology is nothing but a fad, and I'm going to wait it out.
>
> —Rhodeena Culsmucker

Although there is a difference of opinion on some of these ranges, Sherri Elliot-Yeary, author or *Ties to Tattoos: Turning Generational Differences into a Competitive Advantage* (2011), identifies the four generations this way:

Traditionalists. Those born between 1922 and 1945

Xers. Those born between 1965 and 1978

Boomers. Those born between 1946 and 1964

Millennials. Those born between 1979 and 1994 ∎

Elliot-Yeary says there are logical consequences of being born during a certain time period. Traditionalists came of age during the Depression and World War II. They lived in an era when materials were in short supply, and they learned not to waste. The result is a generation of people who are conservative and well disciplined. Their patriotism and loyalty to their country during a time of threat taught them to be faithful, dependable, and respectful. At work, they believe in "paying your dues," doing what you are told, and contributing to the community.

Next came the 76 million Baby Boomers. They were the first TV addicts and the first *workaholics*. Life was easier for the Boomers than for their Traditionalist parents, and many of them developed the belief that they could change the world. They are a generation of optimists and strategic thinkers. They are highly competitive. Boomers believe that long hours and extended effort are what move people forward. They have worked hard to get where they are, and they expect others to do the same.

The children of the Boomers are popularly called the Generation Xers. Elliot-Yeary believes that this is possibly the most misunderstood generation. Xers have had a difficult time separating their identity from that of their parents and grandparents. They grew up during a time when institutions and public figures were regularly and publicly exposed as frauds. Therefore, they tend to be skeptical and mistrustful of any management system. They are generally confident and don't mind asking to move to the top quickly and without "jumping through the hoops." They are the first tech-savvy generation, and they have a strong desire for balance between work and play.

> Never close your door to collaboration. You know how they say that moving elderly people into the hospital can quicken their demise? Closing your door to colleagues is rather like that. The act begins to deteriorate your ability to see the good. When you close the door, you are moving access to positive practices into hospice care.
>
> —Heather Wolpert-Gawron, middle school teacher, blogger (2013)

A multigenerational team of four teachers is gathered for a meeting. During a quick exchange of ideas, Traditional Terry asks people to slow down and repeat what they are saying so that he can write down their responses for the minutes. Xer Xandra sighs and asks him when he's going to join the 21st century and start using an iPad.

Millie Millennial says, "OMG, are you seriously writing out every word we say? J2LYK nobody does that. XME but, Dude, that is seriously lame."

Terry glares at the two of them and continues to write. Benny Boomer interjects, "Okay, let's move on, shall we? We agreed that we need to challenge the district mandate, and we have this school board presentation to prepare. I thought I'd take the lead on this and speak for our group."

Millie answers, "Since I'm the one who made the final iMovie about it, wouldn't it make more sense for me to present it to the board?"

Benny chuckles, "Well, Mille, I hardly think you're ready to take the lead. I mean you're just a first year teacher, and I don't think people will take you seriously. Why don't you wait until you've been in the trenches a little longer before you start speaking up about something the rest of us have been dealing since before you were born?"

Terry nods in agreement. "Besides that, Benny and I are the ones who did all the hard work on this project. You two left early to go to your Lady Googa, or whatever she's called, concert and didn't stick around to help. We're the ones who stayed here day after day working to 10:00 some nights trying to hammer this thing out while you two had to have your *me time*."

Xandra rebuts, "Look, Millie and I work hard, too, you know. It's just that we know how to work a little smarter and not waste time doing things the old-fashioned way. I don't know what the big deal is anyway. The board is just a bunch of old fossils who only care about getting reelected."

Benny argues, "Look, I'm sure the board members will change their minds once we show them how hard we have worked to create something that is better for our students. Also, I'm personal friends with a couple of them, so I think I'm the one who should make the presentation."

Terry adds, "And at least Benny won't go in there an offend people with an arrogant attitude. In my day, young people showed a lot more respect for their elders."

Millie gathers her stuff, exits, and says over her shoulder, "Well, it's not your day anymore, and all I can say is IMHO you can DIY."

Terry asks, "What did she say?"

Benny shakes his head and mutters, "I have no idea." ∎

And now the educational workforce has added the Millennials, another group of 76 million people. Some call them *Generation WHY* because they don't mind challenging authority or the status quo. Their technical skills make the Boomers and Xers look like novices. Theirs is a generation that wants to make a difference, but they want to do it their way. Because they were reared in the "everyone gets a trophy era," Millennials often feel entitled and have difficulty accepting negative feedback.

These different generations grew up in different time periods with noticeably different values. Sometimes, we are quick to label each other because of our generational differences. Jamie Notter (2013) explains it this way:

> For example, the Baby Boomer generation tends to place high value [on] the group or team (or cause or movement), and Generation X, a much smaller generation that had been left to their own devices as they grew up, came into the workplace with an emphasis on independence and work-life balance. This prompted a lot of conflict, with Boomers grumbling about these new employees not being "team players," and the Xers complaining about the incessant "micromanaging." Of course, now those Xers are managing the Millennials (who grew up in a very different, child-focused, and social-Internet-enabled world) and new conflicts emerge, with the Millennials expecting more interaction with higher levels of the hierarchy and more substantive work content earlier in their career.

Just as with mind style differences and extrovert versus introvert arguments, it can be enlightening to consider what generational influences have on an individual. Taking the time to consider the other person's perspective goes a long way toward bridging miscommunication gaps and beginning to form some sort of alliance with them. Before we "vote people off the island," we at least need to try to give them the benefit of the doubt. Deliberate optimists are those who try to see the finest in others and believe that most people are doing the best they can.

You become like the five people you spend the most time with. Choose carefully.

—Anonymous

Gathering information and accepting people for who they are, though, is quite different from actually liking or even respecting them. Working with difficult people can drain the optimism and the energy right out of a person. And true, there usually is that ONE teacher who really does ruin things for everyone (including school leaders, colleagues, and students). So what do we do about that person? Chapter 4 uses deliberate optimism principles two through five to address the challenge of dealing with negative people.

Action Steps for Teachers

DISCUSSION QUESTIONS AND ACTIVITIES

1. Think of a faculty member you don't like or don't feel comfortable around. What are some things you could learn about that person to shift them to a more favorable light in your view?

2. What learning style do you think best describes you? Name some positives and some negatives that are associated with your style. Are they true about you?

3. Do you consider yourself generally an extrovert or an introvert?

   Give examples of why you see yourself that way.

4. Do you have introverts on your staff? What steps should school leaders and other teacher take to make sure introverts feel valued and appreciated?

5. According to Elliot-Yeary, to which generation do you belong?

   Do you manifest the traits ascribed to your generation in this chapter? Explain your answer.

6. With what generation(s) do you best relate? Why?

7. Do you think it's important to understand a person's basic learning style, generational tendencies, and degree of being an extrovert or introvert? Why or why not?

8. What would you like for your colleagues to know about you?

   Do you think they are aware of the things you listed? Why or why not?

9. Take a look at some of the websites dealing with differences in individuals' styles, personalities, and modalities found in the Appendix, page 142. Discuss with the group the ones you found most helpful and tell why.

10. Read "Ten Tips for Improving Interpersonal Relationships" in the Appendix, page 143. As a group decide which five are the most important. Discuss why. Have each group member write one additional way to get along better with others.

Action Steps for School Leaders

1. Purchase the Adult Style Indicator or a similar instrument and set a time for the entire staff to take it and discuss it. Either you or a counselor can guide teachers through a good-natured, fun-filled experience of personal discovery.

2. Create and distribute a calendar that includes the birthdays of every teacher and staff member. Send a card to each one of them on their special day (even over the holidays and in the summer). Encourage staff members to remember each other with a smile or an offer of help on their special days.

3. If you don't already have one, establish a hospitality committee that will oversee team-building events and fun activities appropriate for the staff members at your school.

4. Once a month, provide food for the adults at school as a special acknowledgment for their efforts. It can be as simple as bagels and juice for breakfast or as easy as a potato bar set up in the teacher lounge/workroom during lunch.

5. Provide free coffee, tea, and water in the teacher lounge or in a central location for staff throughout the day.

6. Provide food and/or treats for every faculty meeting.

7. Plan a retreat before school starts or in January. Make sure it is off campus and is in a desirable location. Mix learning objectives with fun, collaborative activities. Provide time for personal reflection.

8. Plan a faculty outing to a roller rink, a bowling alley, a paintball facility, miniature golf range, or some other kind of entertainment venue that will have participants moving and interacting. Probably some won't come, but that's okay. Those who show up will have a terrific time.

9. Ask staff members to provide you with pictures of themselves when they were the age of the students they teach. Display them where both staff and students can see them and let people see how many they can match to the adults at school. You can even make it a contest and award prizes.

10. Set up something like a "Secret Pal" society whereby each staff member anonymously affirms another staff member with small treats, positive notes, and thoughtful deeds. The secret pals can remain the same for a holiday season, a semester, or the year. Have a Reveal Party at the end of the time period so that identities can be revealed and a random drawing can be held to select new pals for the next time period. Don't forget to put your name in the drawing. (And don't assume this won't work in high school. We have seen it work really well with secondary teachers.)

CHAPTER 4

Building Healthy Relationships and an Optimistic Shared Community

Don't try to win over the haters; you are not a jackass whisperer.

—Brené Brown (2013, p.171)

hapter 3 discusses various strategies for understanding our colleagues and for building stronger relationships with them. Chapter 4 considers the thorny issue of dealing with people who are dysfunctional and/or who drain your spirit. It also points out the importance of building an optimistic shared community.

When adults are asked what factors make their work rewarding, most respond, "The people I work with," or something similar. In these surveys, a person's workplace colleagues are repeatedly valued over pay, vacation time, a bigger title, or even paid health insurance (*Employee Job Satisfaction and Engagement,* 2011).

Being attentive to the needs of one's students and developing new strategies for their success are demands that never diminish. Despite the many hours we spend with students, though, they are not our primary workplace colleagues; indeed, they are not colleagues at all. The teachers on our team, in our department, or at our grade level are. They are the ones who will offer support (or not), share our successes and failures (or not), bolster us (or not) when we are down, and celebrate with us when things are going splendidly (maybe—if there's cake involved).

> *You don't ever have to feel guilty about removing toxic people from your life. It doesn't matter whether someone is a relative, romantic interest, employer, childhood friend, or a new acquaintance—You don't have to make room for people who cause you pain or make you feel small. It's one thing if a person owns up to their behavior and makes an effort to change. But if a person disregards your feelings, ignores your boundaries, and continues to treat you in a harmful way, they need to go.*
>
> —Danielle Koepke

Our adult colleagues throughout the school help us accomplish our individual aims and the overall goals of the school. Forming positive relationships with the various collaborators in the building makes the workplace more enjoyable and gives us the energy we need to face the continuing pressures of being a teacher. We can't escape the fact that we all have a psychological need for affiliation. When a teacher is supported by mature and professional relationships, his or her classroom work improves and his or her relationships with the students benefits. Team/faculty discussions are more fruitful when individuals are familiar with other members of the group. Good ideas are brought forward. Positive conflicts are more easily resolved. Because our workplace is where we spend most of our entire day and because real learning is nearly always based on relationships, making these connections is imperative.

Occasionally, some of the grown-ups with whom we relate are not exactly filled with joy. How can one stay optimistic when others complain, criticize, or manifest supreme apathy about their work as educators? How can we build relationships with colleagues who are constantly negative or who seem to want nothing more than to get through the day with as little hassle as possible?

Chapter 3 focuses on the importance of taking the time to try and understand the other person's needs and motivations. Gathering all the information we can about a colleague helps us build an empathy with that person, which according to researcher Dr. Brené Brown (2010) is the only way to build genuine bonds with others. She states, "I define connection as the energy that exists between people when they feel seen, heard, and valued; when they can give and receive without judgment; and when they derive sustenance and strength from the relationship" (p. 19). Realistically, though, sometimes you may feel you have done all you can, and the other person still saps your energy, your passion, and your delight in what you do. It may be time to move on to our principle two.

Minimizing the Impact of Negative People at Work

None of us is able to change another person. Even with the best intentions, it is not possible to make someone love us, like us, or even respect us. How others feel about us is really none of our business. It's their choice. There are certainly things we can do to try and enhance relationships, but in the end, it is really up to them to decide whether or not and to what degree they wish to participate in a positive relationship. Hopefully, we are self-assured enough to make several efforts to include everyone in our positive community, but occasionally, there is someone who just doesn't "play well with others." What do you do about that mean-spirited, antagonistic, negative colleague or administrator?

Once you have identified a person as someone within whose presence you feel small, unappreciated, targeted, or demeaned, the best gift you can give yourself is to put as much distance (physically and emotionally) as you can between him or her and you. We call it "staying away from *talking snakes*." We recommend that all adults treat each other with respect and professionalism at work, but beyond that, it is important to focus on what you can do to control your exposure to negative people. Here are some tips for avoiding the joy-depleters:

 ## Avoiding Talking Snakes

1. Be polite, but share minimal information about yourself, your class, or your achievements. Your success threatens them, and your failures delight them. Keep your conversations with them light and business oriented.

2. In social situations, do not willingly join a group they are already in or they frequently attend. If the negative person is "holding court" in the teacher's lounge, find somewhere else you need to be. Without drawing attention to what you are doing, always try to manipulate your way out of places where the talking snake is present.

3. If the negative person tries to bait you into an argument, take the high ground and use the Stephen Covey line, "I guess we will just have to agree to disagree on that point." Walk away.

4. Do NOT gossip. If you have a trusted friend, you can share your feelings about Mr. or Ms. Negative, but other than that, stay as neutral as you can whenever that person's name is mentioned. Never let students, parents, or casual acquaintances initiate defaming conversations or repeat derogatory information about the talking snakes. Such indulgences are not helpful and will only further drain your positivity.

5. Realize that everyone may not see the person the way you do. Don't force colleagues to take sides. Politely decline with a reasonable excuse any invitations that include the negative person and leave it at that. Let others make their own decisions about dealing with snakes.

6. There will be times when you cannot avoid the person (he or she may be on

(Continued)

your team or teach next door to you). Figure out what you can control and do it. With a polite smile on your face, you can repeat this mantra in your mind, "I may be forced to work with you, but I am not required to like you. I will work with you for the benefit of our students, but you are getting none of the personal real estate I have in my head. I've got more positive things to think about."

7. We recommend that you try to diminish as much as possible the time you give yourself to think about the snakes in your life. In desperate situations, you might consider asking to be transferred to another grade group, wing, or even a different school. You can try to negotiate a different lunchtime and planning period from them. You can park your vehicle in a spot far removed from where the offending party parks and plan your arrival and departure times to be different from hers or his.

8. Focus on your students, your team, and your personal goals. Don't waste energy worrying about what the snakes are doing. (Unless you believe they are harming kids or bullying weaker teachers—then you have a moral obligation to speak up.) Time and energy focused on people who do not want to change is wasted. Try to remain attentive to the people who value and appreciate you. ∎

YOU'RE NOT BEING PARANOID IF THEY REALLY *ARE* AFTER YOU! (BULLYING IN THE WORKPLACE)

Sometimes, it is not as simple as avoiding one or two talking snakes. Unfortunately there are instances when a person with power and/or a group of people are not only negative but actually try to intimidate others. We have spoken to teachers who feel that either their administrator or a certain group of teachers targets them and more or less bullies them.

When addressing the issue of bullying in schools, people are generally referring to the students, but it can also happen with adults. According to the Workplace Bullying Institute (WBI) the term *workplace bullying* encompasses a pretty wide range of situations, but in general, it refers to repeated, health-harming mistreatment of one or more people that can include verbal abuse, offensive nonverbal behaviors, or interfering with someone's ability to get work done. We are referring to actions that go beyond mere disapproval or general incivility. We are talking about grown-ups who pursue other grown-ups in order to do harm.

Beth Plachetka (2014), school counselor in Illinois, was so concerned about the problem of teacher bullying she wrote her doctoral dissertation on workplace bullying in the K–12 public educational setting. She says, "School is supposed to be a safe place for students and staff. Events of staff bullying by other staff are real and debilitating and are often directed at staff who are specialists in the district and have a history of excellent evaluations."

One teacher told us that because she chose to meet with troubled students during her lunch period, she was approached by a group of union members who told her they had worked hard to negotiate an unencumbered lunch period for all teachers, and she was making the rest of them look bad. They asked her to stop doing job-related tasks during lunch, but she refused. Several of her colleagues decided to *shun* her after that. They would not look at her, speak to her, answer her, or in any way acknowledge her presence. She was left out of conversations. She was not invited to events such as a baby shower, an after-school celebration for one of her team members, and even an end-of-the-year party held in a neighboring teacher's home. She said that shunning was a common way for a powerful clique of teachers to keep others in line. She tried to talk about it to her administrator, but his reaction was, "Well, you know there's really no law against people not treating you the way you'd like. Maybe you should just try a little harder to get along with them." She was miserable at her school and transferred as soon as she was able.

It is true that there is no law against incivility or less aggressive forms of bullying in the workplace, but its effect can be destructive and devastating for all involved. Often we are asked, "But what if that negative person is your boss? How can I minimize the effect of a negative superior?" Good question. One young teacher lamented to us about her experience with her principal, whom she described as "the terminator on steroids."

> She never has a positive word to say to me. When I try to talk to her, she doesn't look up from her smart phone she's tapping on. She writes me up for stuff that she lets her favorites get away with. I teach 110 percent most of the time, and the one time I was a little off and gave the kids a free period, she came to observe. She ripped me up one side and down the other on my evaluation. Her pet teacher gives free periods almost every week. She puts me on more committees than anyone else, makes sure I have at least four preps every year, and gives me the worst possible duty schedule. She ignores the grants I've gotten for this school, the awards I have for teaching, and the fact that I was just voted "My Favorite Teacher" by the students. She didn't even congratulate me on being selected. I work harder than any teacher at this school, and no one cares. Sometimes I think I should show up at the last possible minute, do only the minimal work some of the other teachers do, and leave the second school is out. She hates me, and she is doing everything she can to make me leave.

We know that being bullied causes feelings of frustration and helplessness, increased sense of vulnerability, tension, and stress. It leads to low morale and decreased productivity. It is a serious issue. Our advice to anyone in this situation is to adhere to principle number three, **establish what you can control and seek tools and strategies to help you maximize your power**. It applies in cases of oppression.

DETERMINE WHAT YOU CAN AND CANNOT CONTROL

There are definitely steps you can take to alleviate the problem. Some people suggest that you seek help from a superior. We think that should be your last step. Before reporting to the bully's boss, you might try some of these solutions:

1. Remember that it is not fun to pick on someone who refuses to be victimized. If a group of teachers is ignoring you, pretend you don't realize you're being ignored. Talk to them as if nothing is wrong, smile and wave when you see them, and continue to act oblivious to their exclusions. They may get tired of trying to shun you.

2. Find an ally to stand with you. It's much easier to ignore hateful people when you are not alone. (And it's especially helpful if your friend is the coach who used to play linebacker in the NFL.)

3. Make the perpetrator take responsibility for her actions. "Cruella, you failed to tell me the team was having a meeting this afternoon. Did you do that because you are angry with me for disagreeing with you at our last meeting?"

4. If a colleague or an administrator criticizes you, try to see if there is any merit to the accusation, and agree to work on it. Too often we hear teachers argue, "But everyone else was doing it," or "You never say anything to Mr. Socrates when he does that." First and foremost, we need to do what is right by our students. If giving a free period is not pedagogically sound, then it is wrong no matter who else is doing it. The best response to some reprimands is, "You are right. I will correct that," or "I hear what you are saying, I'll work on it."

WHAT YOU CANNOT CONTROL	WHAT YOU CAN CONTROL
1. How others choose to feel about you.	1. How you react to others.
2. How others do their jobs.	2. How you do your job.
3. The friendliness or the lack of friendliness people demonstrate toward you.	3. How you treat others.
	4. How you handle what you are given.
4. Assignments given to you by a superior.	5. What steps you take to alleviate the problem.

5. Confront the bully on neutral ground and calmly say, "Look Voldemort, I've been upset by some things that happened lately like . . . [specifically list your perceptions about occurrences that have troubled you]." Perhaps try the words, "Help me understand what happened here." Don't attribute motive to the oppressor. Just quietly state the facts and report how you felt/feel about it. If there is more than one person involved, choose the least confrontational person to speak with.

6. Make sure that you are not opening yourself up for criticism. It doesn't matter how great a teacher you are, if you are habitually late for school, meetings, and/or class, you give others an opening to complain. Be professional, be respectful, and be vigilant about doing your job assignments. No matter what others in your building are doing, quietly and diligently take care of all your school business before you try to defend yourself. "Okay, I might have been 30 minutes late for my first class, but I stayed here and worked last night until midnight," is no defense.

7. Start keeping private, accurate records of every action and communication from those involved. We're not suggesting that you become Jason Bourne. Just document dates, times, what is said, what is done, etc. Leave out personal feelings, but as clearly and succinctly as possible record what is said and done by all parties (including you). Reviewing your notes may help you put a different perspective on what is going on. Also, bullies are often articulate, manipulative, and calculating. They can sometimes paint a very different picture than what you convey, even sometimes making it appear that you are the perpetrator rather than the victim. Having accurate records will help you state your case to them or to the next level of management.

> . . . A teacher leader expertly and elegantly finds ways to speak difficult truths to people that need to hear them. Not in a negative way. A teacher leaders holds another teacher on the shoulder and says, "When I hear you talk about your kids, it's very negative. The standard that you verbalize you've set for them is very low. I would like to hear you talk about how your kids can do anything. When we give [young] people a reason to reach, they will." That conversation is a very difficult one for professionals to have. But true leaders are not afraid of that conversation because they've opened themselves up to it in their own careers.
>
> —Rebecca Mieliwocki, 2012 National Teacher of the Year (as quoted in Hetlin, 2012)

Having tried other means, you may feel that you have no choice but to appeal to an administrator for help. If, as in the case of the teacher who worked through lunch, your immediate superior is unwilling or incapable of helping, go to the next level. If the bully *is* your immediate superior, go to the next rank beyond his or hers (his or her boss). When you make your case, stick to the facts. The argument, "I work harder than anyone in this school," holds little sway if the principal found you asleep at your desk during your third period chemistry lab. Let your virtues speak for themselves. Reminding people that you were voted Teacher of the Year for your building 5 years ago is really not necessary and does not strengthen your case. Mary Kay Ash used to say, "Nothing wilts more quickly than a laurel rested upon." Just be confident that you are doing the best you can in the situation you have each and every day for your students. Don't be afraid to ask the grown-ups at school to stop hindering that process.

WHEN CONFLICTS ARISE

We are aware of the harmful effects of personal discord and its negative impact on everyone in a school environment. Whenever humans come into contact for long periods of time, conflicts naturally arise. Some are easily smoothed over by a simple, "I'm sorry, those were my hormones talking in the meeting yesterday." Others require more effort to amend. Nearly every school now offers training for students in conflict resolution. Unfortunately many teachers pay little attention to it for themselves. When conflicts arise among colleagues, some of us sulk, pout, offer reprisals, or generally act worse than the students we teach.

If a group of colleagues could be used as "critical friends" who observe, model, and provide effective feedback to one another, enormous growth and optimism can ensue. Positive, effective professional development occurs when an individual teacher is allowed to set his or her own target areas for improvement and is permitted to invite trusted colleagues in to give honest, specific feedback. To empower teachers—beginners and veterans alike—administrators must give them opportunities to feel competent and self-efficacious.

—Debbie Silver (2014, p. 50)

SOURCE: Copyright (2014) National Association of Secondary School Principals. For more information on NASSP products and services to promote excellence in middle level and high school leadership, visit www.nassp.org.

Unresolved disagreements inhibit any kind of ongoing productivity in the educational setting, but especially among teammates. When conflicts arise, they should be dealt with immediately rather than be allowed to fester. Just as they do with their parents, students easily perceive animosity among teachers—even before the dartboard goes up. All the positive thinking in the world won't cover up a single rancorous dispute among colleagues. For some teachers, compliance or compromise is the easy answer, but often contention and resentment remain so there is no real resolution.

The tough-minded optimist believes in the importance of working out disharmony but is often stymied by the lack of cooperation on the part of other adults in the building. Beaten down by the negative input described in earlier chapters, many educators have lost the will to be friendly and approachable, or even a teeny bit social.

Administrators can also feel less than positive as they are stretched to their limits with demands from just about everyone above and below them in rank. Developing a fun and favorable school climate can fall low on her priority list. It is up to the deliberate optimist to make inroads. Team-building activities, shared after-work experiences, and success in common problem solving strengthen the connections among school professionals. An educator's work can be discouraging and stressful; one has to be intentional in providing positive experiences in order to cope.

> As we watch some of our colleagues down sad and angry paths, try to help them, but also find those who haven't gone there yet. Smiles will help keep you aloft, even if the solutions to greater problems are still in progress.
>
> —Heather Wolpert-Gawron, middle school teacher, blogger (2013)

ACTIVELY DO SOMETHING POSITIVE TOWARD YOUR GOAL

Principle four of deliberate optimism for educators requires that we **purposefully do something toward our aim**. We have seen many schools implement powerful strategies to help the adults at school work in a positive, cooperative manner. Here are a few general ideas to get you started toward building positive relationships with your colleagues:

- Start small. Find out what you have in common with one or two teachers on your team or in your curricular area. Build on those commonalities, then reach out to a few more teachers.

- Find something in common with the Eeyore on your team or in the building. Build on that. Maybe you both liked *Star Wars* or hated *Cats* or love cold pizza (you've seen her stealing it out of the lounge fridge).

- If you are already on a team, take steps to revitalize it. This is risky, of course, but it will be less so if you have at least one ally.

- Don't deny that there are stressors in your work (the Pollyanna personality is pretty annoying) but continue to point out—and act in—ways in which you can overcome those stress points in areas where you have control.

- Do at least one unexpected nice thing for each team member each month—a note, a flower for his desk, a bit of verbal support when she's down. If your team is already in sync, use this plan for others in the building who need to be lifted out of pessimism.

- Support your administrator and keep him or her in the loop. Even if you disagree with a decision, go with it. Agree to disagree in private.

- Commit yourself to loyalty—to your class, your team, your administrators and school. You are seen as the "authority" in your community—build optimism, not defeatism (see "Loyalty" in the Appendix, page 144).

Suggestions for Team or Department Meetings

1. Pledge to be on time and stay until the end.

2. Give the meeting your full attention; do not grade papers or check your score on Candy Crunch.

3. If you have an opinion, share it at the meeting, not at a meeting after the meeting.

4. Listen respectfully to others' ideas/opinions. Try to see their point of view.

5. Don't take conflict personally.

6. Once a decision is made, go with it even if you disagree. ■

General Ideas to Make a Team Meeting Successful

- Bring food. A spoonful of sugar (or M&Ms) makes the medicine go down.

- Have an agenda (sent ahead by e-mail is a good idea) and stick to it. Someone should take notes. (Roles can be rotated.)

- Accentuate the positive—about ideas, students, colleagues, actions.

- Instead of venting about a student (or policy or whatever) agree to find three or four solutions for the issue and put them into action. ■

TAKE OWNERSHIP OF YOUR PLAN AND ACKNOWLEDGE RESPONSIBILITY FOR YOUR CHOICES

In his book, *Taming of the Team: How Great Teams Work Together* (2012), Jack Berckemeyer presents an excellent strategy for resolving conflicts among team members. When teams are having difficulty reaching consensus, they can ask each other the question, "What can you live with?" In other words, he gives teachers the

Putting Things in Perspective

One of the seventh-grade teachers comes into the team meeting with tears in her eyes. It takes a while for anyone to get up the courage to remark on her sadness. "What's going on?" the science teacher asks tentatively.

"Oh, I just got back my evaluation from the instructional coach. I just suck!"

"Really? What does it say?"

"It's about that class where the kids got stuff all over the floor because we were cutting and pasting for the poetry wall."

"That class?" says the math teacher, "The kids loved that class—they are still talking about it this week!"

"Yeah, maybe the IC just wanted to remind you about leaving time to clean up at the end—that seemed to be a good class. You don't suck!"

The teacher begins to perk up. "Maybe I'm just overreacting. Thanks, guys." ■

responsibility of making a decision while still offering them ownership of its consequences. A team member might say something like, "I don't like the idea of not letting the students go back to their lockers after each class change, but I can live with restricting visits to the lockers during lunch."

It takes courage to stand up for one's students, but that's what we do every day. It probably takes even more courage to stand up for one's self and one's vocation, and that's where we need to improve as a profession. Principle five of deliberate optimism for educators requires us to be more authentic in our relationships with the other adults at school. We need to support one another, to sustain one another, to lift each other in times of hardship.

We also need to challenge each other, to hold each other accountable, and to trust each other enough to become reflective practitioners together. Speaking up for what is best for kids is part of taking responsibility for our profession. We must constantly reflect as group members how well we communicate with each other as well as how honest we are with each other.

Douglas Larkin (2013) calls candid conversations about how to get better in our teaching an act of *compassionate confrontation*. He says that we should not be as concerned about bruising professional egos as we are about helping each other learn hard truths about our teaching expertise. He thinks the lessons are best learned from trusted colleagues. With a healthy, trusting relationship, perhaps you could expect a conversation like this:

Bad Teaching Day

A group of secondary history teachers are having an informal gathering in the lounge. It has been a hard day, and everyone is just glad it's over.

Dennis chuckles, "Yeah, I kind of hit a new low today. I was so tired by sixth hour that I just handed the kids a study guide, told them to fill it out, and dared them to say one word. And wouldn't you know it, my two worst boys got into it. I had to write them both up and send them to time out. Then four of my other students just shut their books and refused to work, so I wrote them up, too. Man, I don't know what is wrong with these kids."

A couple of his colleagues exchange looks. Jaden says, "You gave them a study guide to fill out for the entire 50 minutes? Seriously? Wow, that doesn't sound like you, Dennis. Usually, you have the coolest activities for the kids to do. You're kind of my hero when it comes to engaging kids."

Dennis replies, "I know, but I was tired, and dang it, all I asked was for these kids to just be quiet and work. Is that too much to expect?"

Lyndon chimes in, "Are you talking about that study guide that comes from the book publisher?"

Dennis nods his head sheepishly.

Lyndon is incredulous, "But, Dennis, isn't that the class with lots of kids who can barely read? I mean, I can see how they got off-task if they couldn't read the text."

Dennis shakes his head, "Yeah, I know. It was a lame assignment. I just didn't have anything left in me, you know?"

Reina says gently, "You know, Dennis, I think we've all been there. I know I have. But later when I thought about how unfair it was to the students, I realized I had to be more in tune with what really works for them. You should have told us you were having a bad day. We would have been glad to step in and help."

Dennis looks around, "So y'all think it was my fault that my kids acted out?"

Jaden responds, "I don't know, Dennis, we weren't there. What do you think?"

Dennis pauses and thinks. He then sucks in his breath and says, "Yeah, you're right. I knew it wasn't the thing to do when I did it. I was just kind of hoping you all would tell me it's okay."

Lyndon slaps him on the back, "Well, you should have known that wasn't going to happen, Dude. We can't ever let you be less than *Dennis-like*, now can we?"

Dennis gathers his stuff to leave. He smiles and says, "Looks like I've got some thinking to do this afternoon. See you tyrants tomorrow!" ∎

Working together, respecting each other, supporting each other, and holding each other accountable are the best ways we can help ourselves and ultimately help our students. Deliberate optimism is not inherent nor is it easy. Dealing with other humans is a tricky business. We need to get to know each other. It helps if we can appreciate each other's backgrounds, experiences, and perspectives. Disagreement is essential to growth, and as long as we can maintain a respectful norm for solving our differences, we can have the hopeful, helpful adult relationships required to do this incredibly intricate job we do.

Action Steps for Teachers

DISCUSSION QUESTIONS AND ACTIVITIES

1. Name things that coworkers do or don't do that drain the enthusiasm and optimism right out of you. What can you do about your loss of spirit when that happens?

2. How have you handled talking snakes in the past? Discuss which methods in Chapter 4 you are considering trying. What other ideas to you have about how to avoid joy-depleters?

3. Discuss the issue of bullying as it applies to the adults in your school. Give an example of a time you felt bullied or witnessed bullying in the workplace. What did you do about it? Were you satisfied with the outcome? Would you do something differently now? Why or why not?

4. Reflect on anything you may have said or done to a colleague that could be construed as bullying. Were you satisfied with the outcome? Would you do something differently now? Why or why not?

5. What advice would you give to a teacher who confided in you that she felt bullied by one of the administrators on campus?

6. Describe a conflict at school among adults in which you were directly involved. What was your role in it? What was the outcome? Would you do anything differently if you could do it over again? Why or why not?

7. Discuss your reaction to the chapter's advice about teaming. What suggestions are you and your team or department already doing? Which suggestions would not work for you? Why not? Name a suggestion you would like to try and tell why.

8. Discuss the piece "Loyalty" by Elbert Hubbard (see the Appendix, page 144) and relate it to how teachers and school leaders should support their schools. Do you agree with what Hubbard says?

9. In the scenario "Bad Teaching Day," what probably would have happened at your school after Dennis made his opening statement? What do you think is the best way to deal with a comment like Dennis made? Why?

10. Name your favorite team-building activity for grown-ups. Tell why you like it and describe how it would work in a faculty meeting at your school. See if you can get your school leader to try it.

Action Steps for School Leaders

1. Provide a detailed weekly memo from the administrative team. This is a great place to add details about upcoming events, give props to staff that went above and beyond, mention birthdays and special events, celebrate good things going on at your school, and reflect on overall goals and school philosophy.

2. With teachers establish common goals and protocols for team and/or department meetings. Drop by their meetings from time to time just to observe the dynamics and to answer questions. Send them a note praising their positive interactions.

3. Listen carefully when someone brings a complaint or conflict involving another person on staff. Ask yourself if this is something you need to solve or if the two people can work it out themselves with a bit of guidance.

4. Try to stay tuned to the dynamics in your building. If the superintendent just gave a talk on how the school board is in a mood to slash the budget, it may be the time for you to bolster morale via a teacher retreat or just hanging around in the workroom offering reassurances.

5. If you know there is a bully in your building, but you can't cut him or her from your roster (they probably bully you, too), avoid punishing that person with onerous duties. Instead, follow the advice in this chapter. You will be a good role model for others, and refusing to be bullied is a great way to irritate the perpetrator.

6. Acknowledge that your faculty and staff have to deal with difficult people both within the school community and beyond. Offer occasional articles or brief seminars to help teachers deal with some of these irritants. Just showing that you are aware of the situation and care about those who are affected goes a long way.

7. From *If You Don't Feed the Teachers, They Eat the Students: Guide to Success for Administrators and Teachers* by Neila Connors (2000, p. 22):

On a weekly form or in personal conversation ask some of the following questions of your staff:

- How was your week?
- What are some successes you experienced this week?
- Did you have any problems this week that the administration team can assist you with?
- Are than any concerns you have about the overall operation of the school?

- Do you have any suggestions for improving the school?

- Do you have any suggestions for the administrative team to improve relationships and strive to achieve our mission?

- Do you have any needs (professional, janitorial, team, etc.) that are not presently being met, and how can we assist?

8. Provide a classroom swap day where every staff member has to take the place of another staff member. Try to put people in jobs as far removed from their "normal jobs" as possible. End the day with a group round-up and ask participants to share what they learned. Design funny questions for them to randomly answer about their day in another job. This kind of activity is great for helping people understand the challenges others face.

9. Encourage positive, cheery teachers to "adopt" a cynical colleague. Have them make it a point to reach out to that person, do thoughtful things for that person, and try to help that person feel more a part of the school community. Be sure to privately acknowledge and offer support to your "Cheer Fairies."

10. Occasionally start professional development activities and faculty meetings with team-building activities that are fun. Plan it so that people have a chance to interact with different colleagues each time. (Ask teachers for suggestions or see "Effective Team-Building Activities and Icebreakers" in the Appendix, page 145, for ideas.)

CHAPTER 5

Creating the Optimistic Classroom
Building a Relationship Culture

[Kids] don't remember what you try to teach them. They remember what you are.

—Jim Henson (2005, p. 47)

C hapter 5 explores the importance of joy and optimism as it relates to the most important aspect of education—the students. Our emphasis is on building positive relationships with them, as well as fostering their healthy interactions with each other. Predictably, teachers who are able to build a positive classroom environment for students actually help themselves in remaining satisfied and resilient. Building relationships is imperative for both the teachers and their students.

THE RELATIONSHIP CULTURE INCLUDES EVERYONE

We strongly believe that educators can have knowledge about their students' various backgrounds, styles, and experiential history, but unless they are able to connect with them in a meaningful way, they will never be able to maximize the teaching/learning process. In other words, regardless of his or her technical proficiency, vast knowledge base, or even monumental expended effort, if a teacher cannot connect with his or her students, he or she cannot teach them. We like to say, "You have to *reach* them before you can *teach* them." And, yes, we are talking about students in PreK–12. Connecting with high school students may not always be as demonstrative as it is in lower grades, but it is no less important.

Secondary teachers occasionally lament that having too many students precludes them from getting to know their students in a meaningful way. It is our contention that if teachers at any level fail to build relationships with their students, they are undermining their success and that of their learners. Perhaps it is reassuring to note that in our current high-speed, multifaceted, prescribed, standardized educational setting, one constant has not changed. Teachers who make the time to build a positive rapport with students will see greater long-term gains with learners. According to Buyse, Verschueren, Verachtert, and Van Damme (2009), when students have a positive teacher-student relationship, they adjust to school more easily, view school as a positive experience, exhibit fewer behavior difficulties, display better social skills, and demonstrate higher academic achievement.

> *Children, in particular, yearn for contact, for belonging to a group. Group membership enables children to overcome feelings of alienation, awkwardness, and isolation caused by a multitude of issues. Incorporating more time for students to talk with teachers and one another is a way to build better classrooms.*
>
> —Brassell, *Bring Joy Back to the Classroom* (2012, p. 82)

The goal is to create a *relationship culture* that is embedded into the climate of the school. It is not something that is done overnight. It takes time, commitment, and strong leadership. Relationship culture is just as important as the academic rigor that schools strive to achieve. The entire staff must understand that there is an essential process and belief about how we treat each other, how we interact with our students, how we engage with parents and guardians, and how we honor guests who enter the building. A relationship culture should be taught and practiced by the students within the building. This culture is not just observed by good deeds and kindness, but also by support and respect for each other. Students want and crave a place that is fair and consistent. For many of our students, school is the only place for them to be treated fairly by adults and their peers. In many cases, educators are the most stable people in some of our students' lives. (We know that this might be shocking to you as you look around the room during a faculty meeting.)

As we stated previously, we need to hold each other accountable in building relationships within the school. We think adults at schools should start "policing our own ranks," which refers to how we hold each other accountable for how we treat students so that we can create a schoolwide relationship culture of optimism and respect for all.

We sometimes think that the easier tasks within a school tend to be elevating teaching strategies and mastering new educational trends. The more difficult tasks are the ones in which we are asked to change our overall beliefs about the humans in the building. If we begin the process of building relationships with students, teaching critical thinking skills, essential ideas, and self-efficacy become far less difficult.

SCHOOL CAN BE A VERY
TOUGH PLACE FOR SOME STUDENTS

Every day, millions of students walk into an institutionalized building that some-times has inadequate heating and cooling, where the rooms smell like last week's science experiment and floor wax—all to be jostled around in hallways that are at times too crowded and filled with oversized backpacks and small cubbies or lock-ers. Some students are greeted pleasantly by their peers, others are ignored or meanly insulted, depending on their place in the underlying social strata that always exists in human societies.

For some students, school can be a sanctuary or a living hell. Just as Matt Groening (2004), creator of *The Simpsons*, illustrates in his cartoon book *School Is Hell*, school can be a harsh place for students. Most educators acknowledge that sometimes our students can be very mean, rude, and cruel to each other. While this can be true for how students treat each other, it can also be true for how teachers treat the students.

Social cruelty among students has existed for centuries. We are sure that Roman children made fun of other students' unclean togas. In our teaching roles, most all of us have witnessed the unnecessary meanness that students can exhibit. It starts at a young age when a 4-year-old takes the toy of a smaller student. It grows into 9-year-olds who talk behind each other's backs, and it becomes ruthless in middle school when cyberbullying and fighting become an accepted extension of a dispute or disagreement. In high school, it can lead to large groups of students tormenting one another.

The noncognitive skills of cooperation, collaboration, respect, and civility are val-ued by every part of society. Businesses tell schools they want students who have social skills and can act as part of a team. Admission committees for colleges and universities look at more than academics when considering a student for enroll-ment. Yet more time and energy is spent every year on test-taking skills than on character education.

OBSERVATIONS ABOUT SCHOOL SAFETY

For optimism and hope to flourish in our learning institutions, we must work to instill a sense of safety among all who are there.

We think it is imperative to apply the Five Principles of Optimism to questions about school violence and its lesser counterparts, bullying and peer conflict. Teachers and school leaders need to determine the actual data about these problems in their schools as they work to circumvent the things they cannot control. They have to understand what they can control and put positive steps in place to ensure that every student has a reasonable expectation of safety at school and school-related events. And they must take ownership of a commitment to address the underlying causes of the problem. (See "School Violence, What Should We Do?" in the Appendix, page 149, for an activity about potential violence in your school.)

What can schools do to promote antibullying, zero violence, tolerance, and acceptance of others? There are many great programs such as Rachel's Challenge (www.rachelschallenge.org), which is being implemented by numerous schools. Good schools offer quality-researched programs to help them build the foundation of antibullying and relationship building, but *great* schools go above and beyond clubs and add-on programs to get to the heart of relationship dynamics. Below are some suggestions to help schools in building a relationship culture that includes everyone.

Ideas for Building a Relationship Culture

1. The adults at school greet students every day as they enter the building. This might mean assigning some teachers and administrators to the main entrances of the school. Some schools greet the students and the parents as they drop their students off in front of the building. We have even seen an administrator and a teacher greet every student when the bus pulls up into the parking lot. (And yes, the educators in the building also wave even more vigorously as the bus leaves school at the end of the day.) Greeting students helps set the tone for the day and helps with security issues. It allows the staff to check on the demeanor and attitude students have as they enter the building.

2. As students enter the building and are greeted, the teachers and administrative team can make sure that every student is also "ready to learn."

This might mean a reminder that the student's shirt needs to be tucked in, the hoodie taken off, the hat removed, and the pants pulled up. (Added note: Do you know what the longest educational trend has ever been? Sagging pants! We are going on over 25 years of sagging pants. Heck, *phonics* did not even last that long!)

3. Expect all teachers to be visible in the hallways saying hello to students. They can do this by their classroom doors and in the hallways. In school observations, we have noted that some educators refuse to greet or even acknowledge students. In our opinion, this is an example of *educational criminality* and is further evidence that we need to police our own ranks by letting all adults in the building know it is not an acceptable practice to ignore kids. In all fairness, we know that many educators are exhausted, disheartened,

and even a bit angry that the educational system has let them down. But here is the reality—whatever is happening to us is not the fault of a student. A 7-, 11-, or 16-year-old did not put us in this situation. We can start by saying hello to our students in the hallways; it is the least we can do!

4. As the educators, we can create an oath or an agreement about the expectations of educators and leaders in the building. This could mean that there is a list of statements that everyone agrees to. Decide a simple and easy way to make each of the statements visible and recognizable. In other words, what ways do we see teachers greeting students, and how do we hold each other accountable when that does not happen? The easy part is making the list; the hard part is holding each other accountable.

5. Making sure every student has an adult advocate also helps create a relationship culture. We discuss ideas later in this chapter as we describe enhancing adult-student relationships.

6. Change or improve the culture and climate of school regarding relationships so that every adult has a chance to know every other adult in a meaningful way. We provide several ideas for team building throughout this book. We also encourage adults to display their educational backgrounds as well. (Yes, it is okay to flaunt your degrees and achievements. We do this for our students and should do it for ourselves.) ■

Not only can teachers and school leaders act collectively to address the deep roots of social problems at school, but we can act individually starting with our own classes. Something as simple as the classic sociogram can be so effective, yet how many of us now take the time to look at how our students fit in the school or classroom culture? How many of us make the time to forge those important relationships not only among students, but also with us? Believe it or not, teachers in PreK all the way through Grade 12 are very important to their students.

One of the authors has a brother who is not a teacher. He had listened for years about all of the extra effort and things his sibling did to connect with students. He would just shake his head and say, "I don't know why you put that much of yourself into it. My teachers never did that, and I did just fine." One day, he called to say, "I will never ask you again why you do what you do. At my work today, I was talking with a young man who confessed that at one time in his youth, he had seriously contemplated suicide. He had it all planned out and was just waiting for the specific day he had chosen. I asked him what changed his mind. He told me

. . . outstanding teachers routinely do what a thousand hand-wringing social programs have found impossible: close the achievement gap between rich and poor, transform students at risk of failure into achievers and believers, and rewrite the equation of opportunity.

—Doug Lemov, teacher, author of *Teach Like a Champion* (2010, p. 2)

that on the day he planned to end his life, a teacher he cared about had reached out to him and told him she was worried about him. She didn't do anything exceptional except listen to him, comfort him, and tell him she would help him work through this. He said that one brief conversation changed his mind, and he credits having been saved by that teacher." The brother choked back tears and said, "That teacher was you, by the way." Then it was the author's turn to cry because that student and that conversation were but hazy memories. Recall of the student had faded, and the exact conversation was not even remembered. The teacher cried because of the thought, "What if I hadn't reached out to the student on that day? I cannot even remember the event, but a life was changed that day, and I didn't even know it. Sometimes, I am overwhelmed by the power we teachers have."

RELATIONSHIP CULTURE: HOW TEACHERS SHARE INFORMATION ABOUT THEMSELVES

What we do or don't do, say or don't say, are or are not, truly matters to students. Each and every day, students at every level are scrutinizing us carefully to see what changes we have made to our hair, clothing, and shoes. (Yes, they know when the roots get done and when we wear the same outfit twice in one week.) It is true that most students cannot see the assignment written on the board behind your head, but they do see (and like to point out) the tiniest spot on your shirt or piece of food lodged in your teeth. In spite of our foibles, though, the fact remains that all students aspire to be an adult. In most cases, who are the important mature adults in their lives that they look at anywhere from 50 minutes to a full day for over 180 days? That would be the perfectly pressed teacher. (Or some of us might call it a good day if we have on matching socks.)

With all the pressures and constraints on our time, how can we make sure that we are still building a positive relationship culture? *Purposeful attention* to relationship building within our classrooms and buildings is a start. Strategies and ideas don't have to be complex or time consuming. Many suggestions can be woven seamlessly into an environment or a lesson that is already established. It can be as simple as sharing some things about ourselves with our students. Here are some suggestions from one of our authors on what a teacher can do to start the relationship building by letting students know more about you:

Sharing the Real You With Your Students

- Have pictures of you, your family, your pets, and your friends framed and placed around the room.

- Bring your scrapbook or old school yearbooks to class for students to view.

- Weave relevant personal stories into appropriate teachable moments.

- Participate in team building and/or advisory activities with students.

- Stock a bookshelf with books you read at their age along with your personal favorites now.

- Make a display or list of people you most admire.

- Perform for them something you like to do such as a dance move, karate move, song, interpretative reading, magic trick, physical feat, or joke.

- Bring in artifacts of your skills like a trophy, a certificate, a painting, a poem, a song, something you built, a needlepoint, a picture of your garden, a picture of you competing in a sport, a picture of you doing charitable work, or whatever it is you do when you are not with them.

- Share with them your "dream list" of things you still want to do in this world before you leave it. ∎

© Debbie Silver, 2001.

It is sometimes the little things that help build relationships with kids, and part of that can be sharing our stories with them. There are also great ideas for getting to know about your students. We believe it is critical to go see them play sports, watch them perform in the band, or sing with the choir anytime that you can. It might even mean attending a few dance recitals, birthdays, and other events. We know this takes time and energy.

The fact is you do not even need to leave the comfort of your own home or classroom to make a student feel special. In some cases, many middle school teams, elementary teachers, and high school teachers are making it a priority to write letters to students and parents about simple and great things that are happening in their classrooms as well as about their child's accomplishments. Personal letters have special meaning and are quite different from the computerized mass-produced letters that clog our mailboxes. Many of us have received e-mails, letters, and handwritten notes from a friend, a teacher, or a parent that have lifted our spirits and changed out outlook on life.

THE ART OF WRITING A LETTER

One author's most memorable and meaningful experiences in life began when his father wrote him a letter every week starting when he entered his freshman year of college. His father would put pen to paper each Sunday to share with his son the highlights of the week and the local weather updates. Even though they lived only 2 hours away and talked on the phone at least twice a week, the letters still came. Even after college and during his teaching career and brief move to Ohio, the weekly letters still came. Now as his father is turning 92 years of age, each letter takes on a new meaning and new sense of worth. They are now words that have value and meaning—even if they just mentioned the weather or a small event that happened in his day. They are memories written by a loving father to a busy and humbled son who still gets excited when a letter arrives. The letters are fewer now, but the four shoeboxes of over 1,300 letters still remain a major part of his son's life.

Thirteen hundred is definitely a lot, but how many students in a year do you teach? Multiply that by the number of years you've been teaching, and you'll have a significant number. How much of an impact would a letter offer to a shy, alienated, or disengaged student? Would they be placed in shoebox filled full of accomplishments and meaningful memories? Each of us as authors has spent time writing and sending letters. Sometimes we never hear back, but sometimes we've received an unexpected call later in life with the all-so-familiar "Ms. Pace, do you remember me?" Sometimes we wonder who we write the letters for—ourselves or for our students? Nothing fills the soul with joy like sitting down and writing your very favorite things about a student. (Yes, even that kid who shows up nightly in your nightmares—maybe especially him.) See "Tips for Writing Letters to Students" in the Appendix, page 150.

MAKING SURE EVERY CHILD HAS AN ADULT ADVOCATE

You may be asking yourself, "Are the authors saying I should be my students' buddy or friend?" Definitely not. That is not our role. We want to be their adult advocates. This should happen in every grade configuration and at every building. For example, Norma Bailey is a professor in Michigan and, in our opinion, is a great example of how one can be educationally rigorous while still setting the tone of being an adult advocate for students. Norma has always pushed the envelope in her beliefs and expectations. She is a good listener and gives the best hugs, but she also makes sure her future teachers are prepared and have the knowledge to become outstanding teachers. If you were to ask Norma what makes her exceptional, she would simply say, "It's about relationships." She knows that in order to make a connection with a student, you first must be willing to be yourself and earn their trust.

"But wait, I teach over 120 kids in a day, how can I make connections and be an advocate when there are days I forget what room I teach in?" Here is an activity that can be done by an individual teacher, team, or grade level.

Index Card Activity

- Write down every student's name on an index card. If you have 120 kids on your team, then you should have 120 index cards. If you are doing this for your entire class, then just write down the names of everyone in your class. Another option is doing this for each class you have during the day. Put the student's first and last names on the index card. Write big so that you and everyone else can see the names on the cards.

- If you are doing this with a group of teachers, place all the cards on the table, face up, with every name visible. If you are doing this by yourself, you can then use the cards every couple of days to connect with your students. Just rotate the cards throughout the week or month.

- Next, have the most experienced teacher on the team choose one student by picking up the index card. Teachers should pick a student that they have come to know; a student that might make them smile; or the student that might make them crazy, but that would make the drive to the insane asylum fun. The idea is to choose a student you have a connection with.

- Once you pick the card, you must explain to the team or the group why you picked that child. Just give a couple examples.

- Have the next most experienced teacher pick a student and explain why. Repeat this three times for each team member. The goal here is for other teachers to hear about attributes in their students that they may not have originally seen.

- Or you can complete several rounds— each teacher picks three names per turn (three or four rounds). Group members do not need to explain why they picked each kid, unless they want to.

- Once there are about 20 names left on the table, stop and have everyone in the group look at the names. Ask, "Why have these students not been selected?" Is it because you as a team don't know the student, or is it because the student is unlikeable or has a behavior problem? Could it be based on some form of teacher bias that we have toward students? This part of the activity is critical. It allows us to face some of the issues we adults have toward students.

(Continued)

- Group and team members make sure every child is picked. (You may have to trade two Bernice's for a Bob and a better pick next year.) Remember the goal is to have every child picked by a teacher. Once you have your set of cards, rotate five to seven of those cards every week. Make sure you make natural connections with those five to seven students. Check up on them, ask them how they are doing, and talk about the weather or sports. Kids need to know someone cares. Please note, don't stop talking to other kids; you will still be talking to them as well. You can do this even if you are not doing the index card activity as a group or team.

There are a couple hints for making this activity work.

- After several weeks, you may need to trade a student to another teacher. A natural connection might not happen for you, but will for another teacher. Feel free to ask the "noncore" teachers (also called "encore," or as we prefer to name it, "essentials," subject teachers—such as the art, physical education, music, foreign language, or band teachers). They can be a great help in advocating for kids. After all, for many of our students, their encore subjects are the best time of their school day.

- If doing this with a group of teachers such as team, department, or grade level when picking the last 20 kids, teachers may not end up with exactly the same number of students. It is not about quantity, it is about quality.

- As a team, reflect on the 20 students that were not picked in the first several rounds and really ask each other why.

- After a while, you can also use those index cards to form team groups and maybe even change your homeroom at semester. It can also help when you go on field trips or just for small group activities. ■

SOURCE: Material adapted and excerpted from *Taming of the Team: How Great Teams Work Together* by Jack Berckemeyer with permission of the publisher, Incentive Publications by World Book, World Book, Inc., all rights reserved.

TAKING THE CARDS TO THE NEXT LEVEL: CARE AND CONCERN

Sometimes, when we really need to help a student out with life issues, academic concerns, or emotional problems, do we purposefully gather the information that we need to paint a complete picture of the student? Some schools are establishing a care and concern process. This can take about 10 days and allows teachers, administrators, counselors, and support staff to observe the student and gather all the data possible about every aspect of his or her life. Once you gather the information, you can then meet to discuss and create plans or interventions to help the selected student(s).

In many cases, we just sit and vent about a student who is struggling or dealing with outside influences. The question remains, does that help build a relationship culture where teachers and administrators are empowered to make decisions and work on real-life solutions for kids? Try going a bit further after collecting your index cards. Write down information about the student that will help with creating real solutions to help with issues. It also helps keep us focused when we discuss this student's well-being with others. Areas you might include are the following:

> *The students in my classroom only have 185ish days to spend with me. I don't want to waste them yelling about things that don't matter. I want them to enjoy their time and learn, so I don't sweat the small stuff. I remember that we have limited time so we should all enjoy it.*
>
> —Kelsey Gill, teacher, Goshen Middle School, OH

SOCIAL ISSUES	EMOTIONAL ISSUES	ACADEMIC ISSUES	OUTSIDE INFLUENCES
• How is the student socially with his or her peers? Does she get along well with others? Has she made a group of friends? And who are some of her friends?	• How does he handle praise and conflict?	• When you review this student's achievement data, what areas are his strengths and what are the areas that need improvement?	• How much support does he have outside of school?
• Is he talkative or more quiet and shy?	• Does she show no emotional connections with you or others?	• Does she have the basic organizational skills and tools to be successful?	• Whom does she rely on outside of school?
• Are her social interactions appropriate for her age?	• Does he cry easily, or is he quick to anger?	• What do his grades looks like for this year as compared to past years?	• Are there home and safety issues?
• How well does he communicate with peers and adults?	• How does she interact with her peers and others?	• What skills has the student shown regarding proficiency and advancement?	• Are there medications or other health issues?
• Do her social issues affect her schoolwork or the classroom environment?		• Does she need some enrichment or remediation to help her become successful?	• Can he count on supportive adults in his life such as parents, grandparents, or siblings?
			• Has there been a recent divorce or other family-related concerns?

We understand there are some tough issues that children face each and every day. Great teachers and schools discuss these issues in a professional manner and then look for solutions in the context of the whole child, not just what is presented to us in our classrooms. For an effective way to get to know your students, practice Judith Baenen's "How to Listen" found in the Appendix, page 151.

What It Means to Advocate for Students

Students of all ages need adults in their lives who pay attention to them, listen to them, and point them in the right direction. Sometimes a brief greeting or question about how the day is going is all that is required to let students know they are valued and that they belong. Occasionally students need the help of an adult to solve a problem, make a plan, or just give some guidance. Depending on the grade, maturity, and skill levels of the kid, educators can step in when necessary to offer an assist.

While we want all students to eventually evolve into self-sufficient independent learners, there are many times it is desirable for educators to offer help. The willingness of educators to advocate for students is an indicator of a positive school community.

 Scenario 1

A student's advocate goes to bat for him because she understands what is at stake.

Jeremy enters the homeroom, tosses his backpack on the floor, and slumps in his chair.

"What's up?" you ask.

"I studied for my stupid science test today, and mean Ms. Pipette wouldn't let me take it because I didn't have a blue pen."

"Gosh, Jeremy, I'm sorry about that. I know you really studied, and when we went over that study sheet this morning, you knew it all."

"Yeah, but a fat lot of good that did! Why should I even study?"

"Look, Jeremy, I'm going to talk with Ms. Pipette and see if you can't take the test after all. I don't want you to give up on studying. I will try to get her to understand that next time you will have your required materials."∎

Scenario 2

A student's advocate assists the student in navigating the everyday problems of being a student.

Mr. Sonnet is waiting in the locker hall when Liza arrives after the final bell for the day. He greets her as she begins to unload her backpack.

"What's for homework tonight, Liza?"

"I don't know—probably math. I don't know."

"How about we look at your planner and see if you wrote anything down for tonight?"

"Okay, if you want to."

"Well, it looks as if you have math and some reading to do in science. You'd better get your science book out of your locker—er, no,—that's your Spanish book; the science book is the blue one."

"Oh, yeah."

"Hey, it looks like you have a history quiz tomorrow. History notes go in the backpack, too."

"Okay. Thanks, Mr. Sonnet. Lots of times I don't get home with the right stuff. Thanks for helping me." ■

Scenario 3

Student advocates help their students plan ahead to ward off possible misbehaviors.

Before the assembly, Mrs. Abuela reminds her students that this assembly today is a serious presentation about an important issue. "This means no stomping feet or yelling like in a pep rally. If you think you can't sit with your friends and remain quiet during the assembly, make a different choice about whom you sit with." ■

Building Student-to-Student Relationships

As we mentioned earlier, students can be malicious and brutal to each other. Sometimes their actions are erratic and beyond explanation. They can kick their best friend's backpack all the way down the hall while calling him or her names, then drop a dollar into the charity bucket for the tsunami relief effort. Many would say that schools and classrooms are like survival of the fittest. The powerful pounce on the weak, and the weak either take the abuse or complain to the adult in the room. The cycle of distrust and disrespect has to be addressed and changed in order to create a positive relationship culture.

The best place to start is by creating a classroom that is warm and inviting to all of our students. It is also a place where disrespect will be addressed and dealt with in a calm and realistic manner. For example, anytime a student is being disrespectful to another student or there is a conflict in the classroom, many teachers are now asking that the students not only apologize, but also to shake each other's hands. The power of the handshake is a lost art that still has symbolic and life-affirming attributes.

Some teachers have their students create guidelines on how to treat each other. They also ask class member to figure out ways to hold each other accountable. Remember that the lists are easy to create; the action items and accountability are the difficult part. See "Student Accountability Sheet" in the Appendix, page 152, for an example.

In order to build quality relationships with students, we need to set high expectations, understand each other, and then hold everyone accountable for his or her choices and his or her actions. One way to really start to build that relationship is to allow students to have a voice in their school and in decisions that affect them. This can be done in various ways such as forming small focus groups with students about topics and issues. There are many reflective activities that allow for student voice and choice.

We know of several schools that have embraced service learning and volunteer work as part of their curriculum. Using the project-based learning (PBL) model, some middle schools and high schools require "capstone projects" that require students to solve a local issue or work within their community to make it a better place. Inspired educators work to provide academic success both inside and outside of the classroom. Here are a few reasons to allow students to use their voices in working within their community or on a project to solve local issues:

School/Community Projects

- Allow students to be seen as a vital part of their community.

- Help with creativity and problem solving.

- Build confidence for the student.

- Help the community see the educational skills and attributes that prepare students for college or the work force.

- Highlight great things that students can accomplish.

- Build affirmative relationships among your community, your school, and your students.

- Give students a sense of voice and choice.

- Sometimes having the community see what tenth graders are like can help build support for you as an educator. It might even help pass local tax initiatives for your school. ■

Creating a positive relationship culture is no easy task. There are many commercial programs now available to help schools improve their school climates; however, we don't believe it's about any program, no matter how sterling. It is about knowing our students, letting them get to know us, and making sure our students feel welcome when they enter the building and our classrooms. For years, we (authors) along with others have said that student learning starts with relationships. The deliberate optimist speaks up and says that schools should be safe havens for emotionally battered students as well as those who are well adjusted, and it is we as teachers who are called to create those sanctuaries. We accept the fact that content is critical, yet relationship building is life changing. If we truly want to reclaim the joy in education, we think we need to be at least as deliberately attentive to students' noncognitive issues as we are to the cognitive ones.

Action Steps for Teachers

DISCUSSION QUESTIONS AND ACTIVITIES

1. What evidence can you cite (it can be anecdotal or something you've read) that supports the authors' assertion that building positive relationships with students supports higher achievement?

2. What systems, programs, or procedures do you have in place at your school that specifically address school aggression? Is there something else you would like to see implemented at your school? What and why (or why not)?

3. Use the discussion guide "School Violence, What Should We Do?" in the Appendix, page 149, to examine proactive steps your school might want to consider in regard to preventing violence at your school.

4. To what extent should teachers share their personal lives with students? Why do you feel this way? How do you share who you are with the kids in your class? As a student, did you like knowing about your teachers? Why or why not?

5. Have you or one of your own children ever received a positive letter from a teacher or mentor? How did it make you feel? Do you write letters or notes to students? Why or why not?

6. What is the difference between being a personal friend to a student and an adult advocate? What would you tell a colleague you thought had crossed the line between the two?

7. What do you think of Jack Berckemeyer's Index Card Activity? Have you done something similar in your class or at your school? How could you persuade other teachers to participate in the activity?

8. What other issues besides the ones listed in the chapter might you want to consider about individual students? How would you go about finding out the needed information that is not readily available?

9. What policies and procedures do you have in place for resolving student conflicts? Are you satisfied with the results you are getting? Why or why not?

10. Name a service project you would like to have your students participate in. Describe the steps you will need in order to implement the project successfully.

Action Steps for School Leaders

1. The administrative team can create its own index card activity, using the names of all the employees (don't forget the bus drivers and other behind-the-scenes workers). Follow the same guidelines for discussion and advocacy for each individual.

2. Don't leave letter writing to students to just the teachers. When you see something great happen or hear of a student success or loss, write a personal note.

3. Try as much as possible to "accentuate the positive." Provide feedback for acts of respect and civility as well as acts of hostility.

4. Engage students in building the school's culture. The more they own it, the more they will monitor it.

5. Ask teachers to take one day during the year to shadow a student. Provide a substitute for the teacher, and ask her to follow a student around for a full day from the bus ride to school to the bus ride home. She should keep a journal throughout the day and spend most of her time listening and watching her chosen student. Have the observing teacher write about the experience, talk to you about it, share with her colleagues, and/or talk with other appropriate staff about what she learned.

6. In a faculty meeting, bring up the topic of student advocacy. Discuss with teachers what you think advocacy means in terms of the grade levels of the students in your school. Brainstorm with teachers a list of "nonnegotiables" about practices for interacting with students on your campus.

7. Set up a few role play situations regarding teachers interacting with students. Draw names or select faculty members to take on the roles of students and teachers. Read a scenario and ask the actors to demonstrate what they would do in certain situations. After the role play, ask audience members to offer opinions about what they saw and contribute ideas for other ways to handle the situation. Move on to the next scenario.

8. Sit in the back of a classroom and imagine what it would be like to teach those students. Make a list of pluses and minuses on being a teacher on your campus. Think about what you are asking your teachers to do. Is it fair and reasonable? Would you be able to do what you are asking of them?

9. Using picture and artifacts, create a graphic display of ways teachers in your school have impacted students, the school, the community, and beyond.

10. Use social networking to arrange drop-ins from former students.

Reclaiming the Joy in Our Classrooms and Our Curriculum

We can no longer use the shield of standards as an excuse not to be creative.

—Rick Wormeli

Chapter 6 focuses on an area where teachers have (or definitely *should* have) autonomy and decision-making power. It summarizes how teachers can restore and maintain joy in their individual classrooms, not only through engaging activities, but also by personalizing their domains. We truly support the notion that as long as teachers are connecting with students in a positive way and their students are learning the mandated essential ideas, they (the teachers) should be supported and encouraged to add their own personal styles to the way they teach. This kind of professional freedom is a sure way to boost morale and maintain a more optimistic climate in schools.

Deliberate optimism can be a struggle for even the most cheerful person. Yes, we're talking about Mrs. Bliss who skips, prances, and bakes brownies. She is an amazing example of how educators can remain joyful even in the darkest of times. And for each Priscilla Perfect or Mr. Magical, we should be grateful, because they're the ones who know that true hope, passion, and optimism still resonate within the confines of a school building. (Plus, they are the ones who bring the all the baked goods and "comfort foods.")

However, not everyone is willing to bake, (and of course—how would you fit that in between grading papers, being a responsive partner and/or overseeing our own kids' homework?). And many of us in the field of education have seen our optimism dwindle over the years—and for good reasons. But we are still in a great profession that allows us to take some risks and spark creativity. "Where are we allowed these freedoms?" you may ask. Well, the answer is easier to find than you might think: It lies in our personal classrooms.

In order to bring back the optimism within your classroom, start by looking at several of the Five Principles of Deliberate Optimism: **gather information, establish what you can control, do something positive, and take ownership**. Of course, any of the five steps can be implemented in whichever order seems most appropriate to the situation.

For example, we may start by **gathering information**. We find that in many of our classrooms in the United States and across the world, there are new curriculum mandates that specify which topic is to be taught on which day and at what time. (In fact, if you are a math or language arts teacher, in the time it took you read the last three paragraphs, you probably missed teaching two benchmarks and a standard.) With mandates that dictate exactly how to teach a topic and for how long, it is no wonder some teachers feel they no longer have educational freedom within their classroom domains.

If we **take ownership** in the situation, we find that as passionate educators, we may have forgotten that our classrooms are where connections are made, imaginations are developed, creative thinking thrives, and wonder never stops. To gain a little more joy and hope, we need to start in the classrooms themselves; your classroom is **something you can control.** It needs to be the ultimate safe place, where students can be explorers, fail and recover, and even learn to question authority.

> Take ownership of what goes on in your classroom. If you blame others, nothing with ever change. If it's your problem, you can solve it. Taking charge of your classroom is empowering because it allows you to move forward toward solutions.
>
> —Julia Thompson

The desire we have as authors is to reignite the power of the classroom. It's not limited to raising test scores with an emphasis on "the core" subjects. We hope to revitalize exploratory classes and to foster classrooms that fire the imagination as well as increase achievement. Maybe some of the ideas outlined in this chapter can inspire creativity and kindle your joy so you can **do something positive.** What you read here should empower you, whether you're a new teacher who just got handed your first curriculum guide or a veteran who has somehow lost your spark along the way.

Start by Making It Look Like *Your* Classroom

Some school leaders are now doing walkthroughs called "Ghost Walks." They visit classrooms when students and the teacher are not present, looking for indicators that individual student needs are being met. None of us (authors) has ever done a

"Ghost Walk," but we have visited hundreds of classrooms among us, and we agree that we can tell a lot about the teacher by how the furniture is arranged, what is on the boards and walls, and what is on his or her desk. We believe that your classroom ought to be a reflection of who you are as an educator and as a person. Since most of us spend more time in our classrooms than in any other single dwelling, we think the classroom should be a place that makes you feel joy just by being there. Make it your own.

When one of our authors works with new teachers, she instructs them that when they get their first job, they should go to the school late one afternoon and move all the furniture out for a short while. She asks them to walk around the empty room and visualize exactly how they would like their classroom to be. Where do they want the students' attention focused? Where do they want to put their personal items? How do they want students grouped? What is the best use of the natural light in the room? When they get a clear idea of what best suits the way they want to teach, they can move the furniture back in according to how it best matches their goals rather than the way it was set up by the prior occupant or how the rooms down the hall are arranged. From the beginning, we want them to realize that this is going to be "home" for a while, and they should make the most of it.

In Chapter 3, we wrote about how teachers have different styles. Some teachers like colorful, lively rooms with lots of works in progress going on, music filling the air, and seemingly very little organization. Others have a classroom that would be the envy of a head librarian with obsessive-compulsive disorder. What is important is that your environment should reflect you, the age group and subject you teach, and the positivity you feel or at least hope to feel. Make it welcoming. Here are a few ideas we've garnered over the years:

1. Bring in pets and plants. If your school has a rule against mammals in the classroom, set up an aquarium. Living things in the classroom make it less institutional. If you don't want the bother of taking care of organisms that are not your students, assign the kids to water the plants, clean out the hamster cage, or feed the fish. Generally, kids love to be in charge of those things.

2. Rooms do not have to smell like Eau de la Gym Socks anymore. With all the fragrance apparati available today, one can easily have the scent of Citrus Delight, Fresh Linen, or whatever reflects who you are and what you like to smell. If artificial fragrances are a problem for you or for one of your students, just slice open an orange at the beginning of the day and leave it near an air vent.

3. Make your room feel less "prisony" by adding rugs, bookshelves, room dividers, beanbag chairs, or other items you pick up at garage sales, yard sales,

(Continued)

(Continued)

or just after Aunt Myrtle's passing. A big rocking chair can do wonders for you or for a troubled student during times of stress (and yes, we have seen these things done in exemplary high school classrooms, too).

4. Hang mobiles, kites, or student work from the ceiling or mount instructional posters overhead. Then at least when students roll their eyes in boredom, they'll be looking at something interesting or educational. We have observed teachers get really creative and cut words or shapes out of heat-proof gels and put them in the plastic covers of the overhead fluorescent lights.

5. Add lamps so you can at least occasionally turn off the fluorescent lights. One teacher we know taught in a room that didn't have a window, so she painted a window on the wall, added curtains, and even put a tiny light to make it look like the sun was shining through. It brightened the entire atmosphere.

6. On the walls and bulletin boards, you can put pictures of students, student work, subject-related tip sheets, seasonal decorations, or whatever suits your style, your subject, and your students.

Some of you teach different grade levels throughout the day or various aspects (e.g., Algebra 2/Calculus) of your subject. Some of you teach vastly different subject areas (e.g., French for periods two and four and Civics periods one, five, and seven). Your classroom has to meet many different student needs. Try creating a section of your wall or board space for each group that uses your room. That's where their assignments will be, as well as articles about the specific subject they are working on, student exemplars, and other information related to their class. When a student from second period enters the room, for example, she will know to go to her section of the board for the latest on her class. This not only provides up-to-date information, it also helps the student create a mindset for your particular subject. (Remember, hearts can be broken at the water fountain, and sometimes, we need to help students reset their learning mindsets when they enter the classroom.)

The point is that it's *your* room, and you should do everything you can to make it a place you feel joyful and at home. Surround yourself with pictures of your students, your family, your pets, your hobbies or interests, and anything that reminds you of who you are and why you do what you do. Remember that teaching is about relationship building. Sometimes taking control over your physical environment is the fastest way to improve your mood and the overall climate of your classroom. If you are not very creative, ask your students or some of your colleagues for help.

DELIBERATE OPTIMISM

THE ART OF PLAY AND CREATIVITY

In his article "The Creativity Crisis" (2010), Po Bronson asserts that there is a crisis in creativity in our classrooms. Bronson and others have found that many schools have lost their desire to emphasize creativity. In fact, he feels without this critical element, we will struggle to solve many of our world's political and economic issues. His article questions whether schools in the United States are so overwhelmed by standards that "there is no more room in the day for a creativity class." Many students are lucky to get a couple of days of art and physical education, let alone time to be imaginative and explore.

This is not true for countries like England and China, which are starting to make creativity a top priority due to its escalating deterioration among students. According to Kyung Hee Kim (2011, p. 293), a researcher at the College of William and Mary, creativity in school children has been on the decline since the 1990s. For many of us, this is no shock. As educators, we have seen a decline in the motivation and imagination that students show in their daily work, projects, conversations, homework, and classroom assignments. Reasons for this decline have been attributed to everything from massive amounts of television time to the lack of play to overemphasis of standardized assessments. There is also the reality that some students simply do not see the value of school.

Yet in the United States, we are witnessing some schools as a whole tackle the issue of creativity. At the National Inventors Hall of Fame School in Akron, Ohio, students are encouraged to solve problems and create new products in ways that align with the state standards. In other schools, individual teachers are building classrooms filled with vividly imaginative ideas. One teacher in Ohio bought four toilets and put them on a small platform so that when students want to read, they can sit on the fake toilet and relax. (Don't worry; there's no water in the tanks—just books for the students to read.) And in one blast of ingenuity, a teacher salvaged the door from an old refrigerator and mounted it right on the wall in the classroom. When students do something they are proud of, they grab a magnet and place it on the fridge. These are great examples of how to **do something positive** and **take ownership** of one's classroom.

BACK TO CONSTRUCTIVISM TO ENHANCE STUDENT ENGAGEMENT

The Bronson (2010) article also suggests that some solutions to student engagement lie in enrichment, inventive thinking, project-based learning, and creative problem-solving pedagogies. Consider other ideas such as the use of games, learning centers, and some good old solid music and movement. Even small innovations can enrich the lives of our students and may provide a little more classroom optimism for both them and their teachers.

Despite the warning of Bronson and others, many of our elementary, middle, and high schools have not done all they can to deepen student learning. In fact, due to test scores and accountability, many of our schools have paid more attention to remediation programs than enhancement classes. Could we be fostering a school climate where we are spending 90 percent of our time, energy, and resources on 10 percent of our struggling student population? As Dr. Phil would ask, "How is that working out for you?"

We believe it is time to revive some aspects of "constructionist classrooms" and "authentic learning." Some teachers have never veered from these ideas, but others have not yet heard of them or dismiss them with, "Yeah—we did that once." Simply put, these concepts promote the view that classroom learning is not a matter of a teacher providing lots of data/information/blah-blah-blah. Instead, students are asked to discover some of their own learning. Teachers guide them into assimilating new learning with prior knowledge and then actually use their new understanding to do something authentic.

PROJECT-BASED LEARNING CAN ADD VIGOR AS WELL AS RIGOR

We are excited by the growing trend toward the constructivist approach of project-based and problems-based learning (PBL). PBL is an instructional strategy that bases learning around a real-world problem rather than on a particular discipline. Both strategies are making their way into K–12 instruction. The idea is to teach students to *learn how to learn.* Many Science Technology, Engineering, and Math (STEM) programs and Science, Technology, Engineering, Arts, and Math (STEAM) programs schools are asking their students to solve real-world problems with critical thinking skills, independent data, and outside resources. By having to solve problems, students practice authentic learning rather than merely memorizing. Not only has research found this practice increases satisfaction in the teaching and learning process, students are actually achieving and retaining more knowledge (Strobel & van Barneveld, 2009; Walker & Leary, 2009).

Students begin with a clearly defined problem that is meaningful to them. They are given just enough information to provoke an investigation. They generally work collaboratively to discuss what information they will need to solve their problem and/or complete their project. Group members are encouraged to work cooperatively with others and use resources beyond the classroom to find the data they need (e.g., Internet, primary sources, periodicals, experts, etc.).

Students use what they have learned to solve everyday problems, to write publishable materials, to debate issues from current events, to create a new or novel approach, devise a computer game, make a presentation, etc. Throughout the process, the teacher provides boundaries and guidelines, but allows students to try, fail, work together, propose solutions, edit with peers, rewrite, experiment, seek out experts, and formulate answers. This type of meaningful, engaging work becomes joyful to students because they have a strong voice in shaping its outcome.

Conversely, some of today's core curriculum instruction is quite the opposite of constructivism. Sadly, some core curriculum classrooms are doing pretty much the same thing every day. The instructional strategies are devoid of opportunities for problem solving, imagining, taking risks, and using one's learning to complete a real-world task. We urge teachers to take control of the mandated curriculum by looking at it not as a flight schedule to be followed to the letter of the law, but as a journey that you and your students will take together.

All of this is just a way of saying that learning should be founded on discovery and should culminate in a meaningful event or task, not another test. Tests are here to stay and can be useful to the teacher for formative assessment and re-teaching, but a test is not always the best measure of authentic learning. Besides, many studies show that students who have gained knowledge via problem solving and working with others retain that information longer. In other words, they will still do well on the almighty assessments (Dogru & Kalender, 2007, pp. 3–13).

LEARNING OFTEN HAPPENS WHEN KIDS ARE HAVING FUN

We are concerned about the lack of *down time* in today's common hurry-up-do-the-work-and-get-assessed curriculum. Making changes toward play and creativity don't have to happen only within the classroom; alterations can be made in the gymnasium, on the playground, or elsewhere in and out of the buildings. For example, some playgrounds now have large wall installations that act like the old electronic game Simon. After the wall flashes a sequence on lighted, colored panels, students run and jump to touch the panels and repeat the series correctly.

In some gym classes in middle and high schools, students are no longer expected merely to bat, kick, or bounce a ball; they also learn about lifelong fitness. Students are given a fitness watch that records the number of steps and calories they burn during class. So, what does the new physical education classroom look like? During a kickball game, students are in the outfield moving and jumping to increase steps and to burn calories. You might even see students moving around as they wait to bat or kick a ball. Creativity and play can be implemented well beyond the borders of a classroom.

Regarding play and unstructured time, we are seeing even our prekindergarten and kindergarten teachers feeling the pressure of standardized curriculum. After speaking to several early elementary teachers, we understand that they feel like the word *play* is sometimes considered a dirty word or a something that must be justified with ten outcomes, a rubric, and a summative assessment. Zosia Bielski (2012) believes that children today are overscheduled and have less time to cultivate a fertile imagination. Without time for whimsical play, children can struggle with managing their emotions and even exhibit a decline in cognitive skills.

In many cases schools have stopped providing recess. Reasons can range from supervision issues to no time within the day and more frequently, to safety concerns. Some educators and parents feel that the lack of unstructured time, such as recess, leads to children playing more combative games, which can lead to developing aggression. Have we started to take away some of the critical aspects that make schools unique and different?

Several years ago, one of the authors was teaching physical education. He occasionally started class with five random items in a box (e.g., a base, a wiffle ball, a volleyball net, one softball glove, and a stopwatch). He handed the box to a small group of students. The challenge was to invent a game using just those items, then teach it to another team and play it. This activity is all about the art of play and letting kids be creative. In today's schools, many students would first ask for a set of printed instructions before attempting such a task. But throughout the building, it should be okay to have some lessons without four stated outcomes and a rubric— activities that allow kids just to be kids!

Too narrow a focus on compliance on a daily basis does not create an atmosphere for innovation or creativity. Joyful teachers are finding ways to bring back play, creativity, and imagination. In many cases, it starts by changing the face of our curriculum and even our school culture.

THE PROMISE OF REINSTITUTING THE ARTS IN OUR CURRICULUMS

Beyond the classroom, level teachers can elicit help from school leaders in providing curriculum shifts that will spark excitement into our schedules. For years, schools have been offering many of the same elective or encore classes: art, physical education, and music. Even though students are spending less time in these classrooms, they're still offered in most schools. We believe that it is possible that we have diminished the arts and electives for the sake of assessments. We often pull students out of classrooms they love only to "punish" them with more remediation and test-taking strategies. We are compelled to ask, what is the overall cost to our society and to our culture?

The great Irish author George Bernard Shaw said that without art, "reality would make the world unbearable." For many students, their classes in art, music, drama, journalism, P.E., and other electives are the only reason they come to school. Education of the whole child is so much more than merely what is represented on standardized tests and a uniform curriculum. Take a look at this interesting summary of what The Music Achievements Council (Music Education Online, n.d.) wrote about teaching music:

Why Music?

1. Music is Science.

2. Music is Mathematical.

3. Music is Foreign Language.

4. Music is History.

5. Music is Physical Education.

6. Music Develops Insights and Demands Research.

7. Music is all these things, but most of all, Music is Art.

That is why we teach music: not because we expect you to major in music. Not because we expect you to play or sing all your life . . .

But so you will be human. So you will recognize beauty. So you will be closer to an infinite beyond this world.

So you will have something to cling to. So you will have more love, more compassion, more gentleness, more good—in short, more Life. ∎

We realize that in most cases, teachers don't have control over whether or not your school or district initiates or reinstates the art class or music appreciation. You can lobby for the arts, but much of this area of decision making is out of your control. What you can do is infuse the arts into your classroom. One high school in Colorado designed an outdoor learning space through a collaborative effort of teachers in the math and science departments. The students used their math skills to create the spaces and then researched which plants, etc., would best work in their environment. In that same high school, music and art are integrated into a tenth-grade study of civilization. Often, such integrated units give other teachers ideas, and they begin to devise ways to mix things up. Teachers also appreciate how much fun it is to plan together and share the work.

CURRICULUM MAKEOVERS WITH ENCORE (ESSENTIALS) CLASSES

Great schools are reimagining elective classes to spark more creativity, increase achievement, and focus on modern life skills. In the article "Why Johnny Can't Sing, Dance, Saw, or Bake" (2013), Jack Berckemeyer suggests one way to start changing attitudes toward electives is to begin calling the classes what they really are—*essentials* (or at the very least, *encore*). You can't say that it is not essential for kids to sing, dance, saw, and bake. These are life skills that help develop a good human being.

Changing the name is just one step in the right direction. The Principles of Deliberate Optimism have taught us to **establish what we can control** and **do something positive**. Beyond using the term *essentials*, great schools are looking at more creative options for their students. And for heaven's sake, let's try not to move backward like the schools that have chosen to offer keyboarding so that students can get through their computerized assessments more quickly.

A middle school in Pennsylvania now offers a class on growth and development and allows students to work with young children in a daycare housed in the same building. This assists students with learning real-life skills they need and teaches them about care and compassion for others. Similarly, some high schools are working with senior centers and daycare providers to allow students to do specific work with children and seniors. More and more schools are offering career technology classes beyond auto mechanics and cosmetology.

Sometimes in order to develop quality essentials classes, we must first look at what students need and want. This allows for student voice and choice within the classroom and school setting. In an international school in Incheon, China, as well as in cutting-edge high schools across the United States, there are classes offered on advanced robotics. Some schools have a functioning audio-visual department run by students with an actual news station that incorporates the latest techniques in animation and video production.

So that they could expose students to a vast network of topics and life skills, one school in Ohio has implemented and mastered "mini-courses." Mini-courses—offered weekly, monthly, quarterly, or once a year—are student focused, have high appeal for students, and help increase social and developmental skills. Classes are hands-on and often relate to health and wellness, sports, gaming, problem solving, and other areas. The range of topics is as vast as the creativity and knowledge of the school staff and as realistic as the opportunities a school desires to offer its students. Here are just some of the subjects currently being offered:

- Gardening and landscaping
- Fishing
- Baking and decorating
- Creating a theme-based movie (zombies are really popular right now)
- Jewelry making
- Auto repair
- Raptors and reptiles

- Zumba
- K'nex and Legos
- Sewing
- Toothpick and trash art sculptures
- Woodworking
- STOMP (making music with trash cans)
- Creating murals
- CSI investigations

Clearly, these are amazing ideas that can foster creativity and ignite the love of learning for both students and teachers.

THE POTENTIAL OF TECHNOLOGY

Inventive Traditionalist, Baby Boomer, Generation X, and Millennial teachers are utilizing technology to inspire originality and imagination in their learners. Programs such as *Study Island* (www.studyisland.com) and *Khan Academy* (www.khanacademy.org) are showing promising results for students. The Internet can even help teachers find research grants that offer funds to help them integrate programs, apps, and technology devices into their curriculum. For a start, check out the listings at www.edutopia.org/grants-and-resources. See also our "Strategies for Writing Award-Winning Grants" in the Appendix, page 153.

Education technology consultant Dedra Stafford (n.d.) recommends the "show-what-you-know" apps and websites, Educreation and Show Me. She suggests Nearpod and Showbie for making the 1:1 environment successful in the classroom. She says, "When it comes to technology in general, educators are constantly looking for websites, hardware, and software that give students the 'lean in effect' whereby students lean in to learn the content so that they can create their own understanding of the knowledge and can retain it far beyond the bubble test. Technology is just one tool, but a powerful one, that does just that."

The biggest challenge in dealing with technology is addressing the barriers we have set as a community and as individuals. While some school districts are working nonstop to block websites, restrict personal devices in the classroom, and limit technology to only time spent in computer labs, Maine has an initiative that provides laptops to students in middle and high school (www.maine.gov/mlti). They encourage learners to use their personal computers for most classroom and homework assignments.

As consultants, we have seen the positive results of encouraging students to use cell phones to respond to teacher prompts and to each other. They can be used for immediate research, for recording a demonstration, and for taking notes. Yet some schools still prohibit them in the classroom. Teachers complain that they are blocked from websites they need for themselves or for their students to access information about important topics. Why are we not spending our time showing learners how to use available technology in a responsible manner rather than asking teachers to spend their time being the *technology police?*

Integrating technology into classroom instruction has revived the passion for many veteran teachers (Magaña & Marzano, 2013), and it offers a familiar path for younger teachers, who were reared on instant access to knowledge of all kinds. An exciting new approach to learning is called **quest-based learning** (QBL). It is an instructional strategy that relies on elements of game design to support student choice within the context of standards-based curriculum. Students select their own activities, called quests, and have the autonomy and leverage to navigate the curriculum as they construct their own knowledge while working toward achieving the desired standards. Originally designed for use in universities, QBL is finding success with K–12 students.

For every inspiring technology story we have witnessed, though, we have also seen students who have learned to despise the instruments that are supposed to free them. As one student in Ohio put it, "Are we getting on the laptops again so we can take another assessment?" We call that another example of *educational criminality:* We have taken a great learning tool and ruined it for our students.

Learning Centers: From Dittos to the Digital Age

Many of us can remember using learning centers in our classrooms. Some of us might even remember them as students. The concept, however, has come a long way. In the past, listening to a song on the tape deck or record player (Millennial teachers may need to look those up with their Google Glasses) was the highlight of our day. (And who can forget those amazing headphones—big and blue, with an antenna on the earpiece that made you look like a character from a Saturday morning cartoon?) Thanks to technology, the learning centers today offer so much possibility: Here are just a few possible ways to use them in PreK–12 classrooms:

- As places where remediation and enhancement can be accomplished
- As opportunities for students to learn at their own pace
- As technology-based learning with gaming and apps that inspire intense student interest and rigor
- Where videos and segments from Khan Academy and other web-based free services can extend knowledge or review ideas
- Where YouTube clips can help reinforce learning

- As opportunities for students to create learning simulations and games to show proficiency and Common Core knowledge

- Where hands-on experiments can foster imagination and exploration

- As places to broaden concepts using Gardner's Multiple Intelligences and Bloom's Taxonomy

- As options to practice listening, speaking, reading, and writing opportunities that help with 21st century skills

- As chances to make mini-movies to show comprehension and to help meet benchmarks

The use of learning centers can increase student motivation and achievement. Isn't it our goal is to produce classrooms where students take increasing responsibility for their own learning? Wouldn't it be great if the teacher not only provided less direct instruction but also became the facilitator of learning? The hardest part is letting go and helping students internalize the self-monitoring and discipline skills they need to stay on task and complete the assigned work, but the end result can be quite invigorating.

CREATING AN ATMOSPHERE FOR LEARNING CENTERS

There are several methods for incorporating centers within a classroom. Use some imagination; explore the structure and content of each center. Don't be afraid to take risks and seek help and support regarding content and technology. There are academic coaches, department chairs, and technology teachers who are all willing to lend a hand. William Wheeler, an innovative technology teacher in Ohio, puts it this way, "We may not have all the answers, but we can help with the resources and tools to make it student focused, age appropriate, and achievement based."

 Types of Learning Centers

- **Rotating Stations.** Students or groups of students rotate through activities.

- **Individualized Stations.** Students or groups only use the stations they need or are assigned to.

- **Sequential Stations.** Students must work through the activities in a particular order and proceed with mastery.

- **Thematic Stations.** All activities are set up to support a specific unit of study.

- **Enrichment Stations.** Areas can be selected after assigned stations are completed. ∎

SOURCE: Cindy Blevins, handout and presentation, NMSA Conference, 2007

ORGANIZATION AND EXPECTATIONS

The initial concerns that teachers have about exploring learning centers are generally how to get started and how to keep the students focused (so that there's no uprising of angry or off-task students). First, start simple. Offer one or two centers and have students work in pairs or small groups. You can even divide the class in half and have one half work on the center. Some of your students might have taken part in learning centers in preschool and elementary school, so some of your groundwork may have already been laid. Start by just offering the centers several times a year; you don't want your students to become bored with the concept. Next, set clear expectations for students on how they work during the center time and allow for a few quick breaks. The best way to make sure students are on task and completing the assignments is to have them self-monitor and evaluate their progress and time. Don't forget to set up guidelines for staying on task and completing assignments on time.

Ideas for Self-Monitoring and Self-Discipline

- Put clearly labeled directions in each center. Laminate everything that's possible (including the directions).

- Use blogs or interactive journals in the center to prompt creative thinking.

- Develop task sheets that students fill out to help document accountability. Sign-in sheets, logs, and charts help with record keeping.

- Students can earn bonus opportunities if they complete the task and work well with others.

- Be vigilant about moving around the room, interacting with students, and showing interest in what they are doing.

- Assign each center a limited amount of time—this helps keep things moving so students don't get bored or off-task.

- Encourage students to help create, add to, and improve centers.

- Whenever possible, use volunteers to help create, manage, and monitor centers. Parent volunteers, preservice teacher observers, and supervisors make excellent center helpers (as do students assigned to "time out," in-laws who need something to do, college-age children home on break, and friends who owe you a favor). ∎

CLOSING THOUGHTS

Of course, there are thousands of other great ideas for teaching strategies that could fill countless books. Yet teachers are notorious for being nonreaders, especially in their field—education. If you are reading this book, you do not fit into that category, but you know full well that many of your colleagues seldom read about their profession. The multitude of ideas in journals, online, or even in the classroom next door are lost to them.

If you are an administrator or team leader, we suggest that you select one article per month to be copied and distributed. Teachers are more likely to read one article than pick up a journal (unless there are great cartoons). You could even run a quick contest using the article—answer these three questions and get a free specialty coffee drink or a free slice on pizza day. If you find a great article online, send the link to your staff or colleagues. Give them an idea of how long it will take them to read it ("This is just four minutes of your time—and well worth those minutes!"). Encouraging them to read timely, to-the-point, and enriching pieces that will immediately help them in their classroom will go further than the latest research on frontal lobe paresthesia.

Our goal in this chapter is to focus on general strategies and a few new or renewed ideas for teachers to try. Just remember: Establishing a joy-filled classroom starts with the internal desire to do what is best for your students. It also means taking risks and empowering yourself to create and to inspire. Using the shield of standards as an excuse for mind-numbing instruction is unacceptable. Uninteresting lessons destroy optimism for both the students and the teacher. Perhaps you can't solve all the educational problems with a really cool room and engaging lessons, but it's a great place to start. And once you start, you'll continue to find new ideas and solutions that can spark your own love for learning.

> *No student deserves to have a teacher who has given up hope.*
>
> —Richard Curwin (2013)

Your optimism will also help your students and colleagues move closer to experiencing a sense of fulfillment and enjoyment. So take the risks and remember that your classroom is still your domain, and within those walls, amazing things are possible.

Action Steps for Teachers

DISCUSSION QUESTIONS AND ACTIVITIES

1. Explain what you think Rick Wormeli means when he says, "We can no longer use the shield of standards as an excuse not to be creative." Do you agree or disagree with that statement? Why or why not?

2. Identify some of the major shifts in education that have impacted your class in the last 5 years. Were the effects positive or negative? Why?

3. If people you have never met did a "Ghost Walk" through your class tonight, what would they be able to say about you as a teacher? Why?

4. Read the poem "Student-Centered Teaching" in the Appendix, page 154, and discuss the importance of continually adjusting your teaching methods to serve the needs of learners. On a scale of 1–10, where would you rate yourself as a student-centered teacher? Would you like to be more student-centered? Why or why not?

5. How do you feel about Po Bronson's assertion that there is a creativity crisis in our classrooms? Argue either for or against his opinion and cite examples to back up your position.

6. Why have so many schools cut recess out of their curriculums? Do you agree with this idea? Why or why not? What can we teachers do to ensure that our students get some "down time" during the day?

7. Are you satisfied with the essentials (electives) offered at your school? Why or why not? How would you propose to maintain the status quo or change it?

8. What are your biggest challenges in using technology as a powerful tool in the classroom? What steps can you take to address those challenges?

9. Describe a powerful learning center you have used in your classroom or witnessed in another teacher's room. How was it used to enhance student learning? How did the students interact with it? Could it have been even better? If so, how?

10. Plan and present to your group a model of a learning center you would like to use with your students. You can draw it, build it, or capture elements of it from the Internet. List your objectives for the center, describe how students will interact with the center, and discuss how you will assess the effectiveness of the center. Be creative and be you.

Action Steps for School Leaders

1. Within reason (and always with an eye to safety), let teachers have as much freedom as you can in setting up their classrooms. Painting walls, moving furniture, and decorating to taste gives teachers a sense of autonomy as well as a place to call their own. Their style may not be your style, but uniformity is usually not joyful.

2. Provide opportunities for teachers to visit each other's classrooms on a regular basis. Set up a schedule so that they can observe other teachers (individually or as a group) and then provide feedback and/or ask questions of the teacher. Some schools do this in a similar way that interns often "make rounds" to learn from other doctors.

3. Provide opportunities for small groups of teachers to visit other school campuses. In a faculty meeting, have them share pictures and describe what they observed.

4. Encourage teachers to select and attend conferences and other professional development activities that appeal to their interests. Whenever possible put together a group of teachers who want to go to the same event, and you go with them. Attend sessions with them, dine with them, and travel with them. Learn right along with them so that you can support them as they try new strategies and tools in their classrooms.

5. Set up a designated research area for teachers. Stock it with professional journals, books, and a computer that has connection to a subscription service (e.g., Eric) for downloading journal articles.

6. Maintain a cloud-based inventory of onsite resources and materials for teacher access. Often times teachers have no idea about what resources are available either because they are stored in an unorganized manner or some colleague has checked out certain materials and hoards them in her classroom all year.

7. If teachers on your campus are not familiar with or comfortable with problem-based or project-based learning, arrange for them to attend a conference about them and/or bring in a consultant who can work with them in an ongoing capacity. Having an expert regularly visit, answer questions, and provide support lets teachers know that PBL is not just the next "flash in the pan" strategy, and you are serious about its implementation.

8. For middle and high schools, it may take some selling to get teachers to embrace learning centers as an instructional tool. Plan a professional development for teachers to hear from a consultant at their grade level who can

show examples and talk about their effectiveness. Provide time and materials for teachers to start working on centers for their classrooms.

9. Drop in classes on an informal basis as often as possible. Ask students about their work, and let them show you what they are doing and tell you what they are learning. In joyful schools when administrators enter a room, the momentum is unchanged. Students and teachers are comfortable with having their principals "join the fun."

CHAPTER 7

Balancing Your Life to Promote Optimism

A man too busy to take care of his health is like a mechanic too busy to take care of his tools.

—Spanish proverb

This chapter is devoted to the topic of perpetuating our optimism by making smart choices about how we care for our individual selves. It seems simplistic to state that in order to take care of others, educators must first take care of themselves, but many in our field make truly unhealthy choices in our lives as we skip meals, forego sleep, work incredibly long hours nightly and on weekends, and generally put every ounce of energy we have into our jobs.

In a career that often times requires us to be selfless, more often than not, teachers see themselves as caretakers and encouragers. We get so busy taking care of everyone else that we often neglect our own self-care. Too many times we put our own needs last and tend to think of those who put effort into taking care of their physical, psychological, spiritual, mental, and social needs as being a bit self-absorbed and even selfish. Nothing could be further from the truth. Burning the candle at both ends will eventually lead to complete and total burnout, and we have too many excellent teachers leaving the field already. **Taking care of oneself is probably the least selfish thing a teacher can do**.

Because studies have shown that teaching is a stressful career that can lead to teacher burnout (McCarthy, Lambert, O'Donnell, & Melendres, 2009), it is imperative that we learn to mitigate stress factors with intentional steps toward more balance in our lives. Following the Five Principles of Deliberate Optimism, teachers must be aware of their personal needs, learn which factors that affect their health they can control, do the things that positively impact their welfare, and take responsibility for ensuring their own well-being.

We realize that we are writing about things that most of you already know. Our attempt in this chapter is not so much to *inform* you as to *remind* you how important you and your health are. We hope you will be able to relate to what we are saying, remember to take care of yourself, and even smile as you read some of our rather irreverent examples.

USE HUMOR TO HELP MANAGE STRESS

The first part to managing unwanted stress is to be aware of our stressors as well as our body's reaction to them. Because traditional work stress inventories ask things like "Do you try to do more than one thing at a time?" and "Are there a lot of deadlines in your work?" we find most of them useless. Their stress indicators read like our job applications. Therefore, one of our authors put together the following stress analyzer for educators.

Top 10 Ways You Know You Are an Educator Under Too Much Stress

1. You take the same packed briefcase, backpack, tote bag, plastic crate, or cardboard box full of stuff back and forth to school each day without ever *touching* the contents inside.

2. When confronted by irate parents, you introduce yourself as someone else and pretend you can't speak English.

3. Your idea of a balanced diet is a candy bar and a sugar-free soda for lunch (and/or breakfast).

4. You have nightmares all night about school and the next day take it out on the students who misbehaved in your dream.

5. You chase strangers' children down the aisles at the grocery store yelling, "We don't run at Krogers!"

6. You endlessly pop bubble wrap because you can't afford therapy.

7. You take two aspirin with your coffee every morning . . . just in case.

8. You leave footprints on the students' backs when the bell rings at the end of the day.

9. You slap a teammate and yell, "Bee!" when there really isn't a bee.

10. On the first day of school you proclaim, "One down, 179 to go." ∎

© Debbie Silver, 1995.

If you did not laugh or even smile at this satirical stress analyzer above, it might be a sign that you truly are under too much stress. Loss of sense of humor is an indicator that one is overwhelmed and drained. Humor is a staple when it comes to dealing with stress. You don't have to be a stand-up comedian to make it work, but you do have to be able to appreciate the irony in life as well as chuckle at some of the insanity we all face. Laughing together is one of the best ways to build your immune system, relax your body, lift your spirits, and build relationships. Good-spirited inclusive humor in a school can make all the difference in the world. A sense of playfulness among the adults is great for adult attitudes and relationships as well as a delight to the kids who watch our every move. For an explanation of the difference between inclusive and excluding humor, see the Appendix, page 155.

STRESS AND PHYSICAL WELL-BEING

Our lives are an array of situations that demand a response to change. Some of the stress in our lives acts in a positive way to push us further, to give us energy, to help us anticipate new events. Weddings, births, vacations, graduations, and holidays cause us stress, but usually in a good way. According to The American Institute of Stress, the term *stress,* as it is currently used, was coined by Hans Selye, who in 1936 defined it as "the non-specific response of the body to any demand for change." Later Selye realized that his term was being used synonymously with negative connotations, and he attempted to clarify that stress can be a positive force.

Preparing to meet a class on their first day of the school year, interviewing for a new assignment, hoping that a student will finally reach a much anticipated milestone, and praying for pizza in the lunchroom rather than *canned meat product* are all examples of an excited tension that is not necessarily bad. Our days are filled with small and large occurrences that cause us stress. Most of these situations are not detrimental to our health. However, too many changes at once, major objectionable events, catastrophic disasters, unrelenting innocuous disturbances, and/or any combination of these can cause stress that undermines our physical well-being, our mental health, our personal relationships, our optimism, and our joy.

LISTENING TO YOUR BODY

One of the criticisms of Western culture is that we tend to ignore even very clear signals that our body sends. Rather than in the Eastern way of "Eat when you're hungry, sleep when you're tired," we try to regulate our meals and bedtimes with what is dictated by our schedules or the clock. We say things like, "I can't be hungry; it's only 10:30 am." "I can't possibly be sleepy. It's only 8:30 pm, and I've got way too much to do to go to bed now." We have learned to turn a deaf ear to messages from our bodies.

Scientists tell us that our bodies send us very clear messages when we are under too much negative stress. Different people have various reactions to stress, but these are just some of the ways our bodies try to warn us: headaches, irritability, fatigue, feelings of hopelessness, depression, anxiety, boredom, ulcers, frequent colds, sleeplessness or too sleepy, pain in neck and back, pain in joints and muscles, weight gain or weight loss, cardiovascular problems, gastrointestinal problems, high blood pressure, absenteeism, apathy, disregard for appearance, lack of energy, mood swings, paranoia, increased use of drugs or alcohol, and loss of sense of humor. Do you recognize any of these signals? Are you aware of when your body tries to alert you that it is in trouble?

Stress and burnout are major factors in the reason teachers leave the profession (Ingersoll, 2012). Excessive stress also negatively impacts the lives of those who stay in the classroom. In order to retain a sense of hope and a spirit of optimism, educators have to find a way to experience the joy of working hard in the job they do and to minimize the disruptive influences of overwork, underappreciation, and loss of esteem and self-efficacy in their profession. Being able to balance work demands and personal life is usually best exhibited by people who take very good care of themselves. Doing for others is good to a point, but neglect of self is neither helpful nor virtuous.

> Teachers are human. Teacher time and energy are finite resources. Kids deserve teachers who will work tirelessly to help them reach their full potential. They also deserve a mentally healthy teacher who wants to be in the room with them and has the emotional reserves to show compassion when they need it. This means that—despite what the movies suggest—it is actually counterproductive for teachers to take a second job to buy books or pull all-nighters planning field trips. It also means that schools and districts should plan around using teacher time and energy wisely.
>
> —Roxanna Elden, NBCT teacher, speaker, and author

THE MYTH OF MULTITASKING

We educators take great pride in being able to do more than one thing at a time. We boast that we can take roll, write today's objectives on the board, sign absentee slips, provide hall passes, sell cheerleader ribbons, take up homework, e-mail a parent, text a colleague, fill out an office form, swill a cup of coffee, find a lost textbook, settle a student dispute, feed the class iguana, focus the LCD projector, check for dress code violations, monitor the hallway, and prepare our anticipatory set for first period simultaneously during the 5 minutes of homeroom. New teachers are often overwhelmed by the amount of menial tasks that must be completed before the first class even begins. They watch veteran teachers seemingly handle dozens of tasks without even breaking stride and wonder if they will ever be able to manage all they have to do. How do they do so many things all at once? The truth is—they don't. Almost no one can effectively and productively manage multiple tasks at the same time.

Research in the past few years clearly indicates that when we attempt to *multitask,* we do our work less effectively and less efficiently. In 2007, Massachusetts-based psychiatrist Dr. Edward Hallowell, who specializes in the treatment of attention deficit/hyperactivity disorder, wrote the book *Crazy Busy*. In it he calls multitasking a "mythical activity in which people believe they can perform two or more tasks simultaneously" (p. 18). He argues that rather than multitasking, individuals are actually multi-switching among undertakings. He explains that the more the brain has to think about and make decisions about a task, the harder it is to make the switch.

Several studies have found that multitasking can actually result in us wasting around 20–40 percent of our time, depending on what we're trying to do.

Time management consultants often recommend that people use *layering* to get more done in less time. Understand that layering and multitasking are not usually the same thing. If you start your printer printing a lengthy handout, set the filter on the fish tank to self-clean for the next 30 minutes and begin filing papers while you have your phone on hold waiting for a parent to pick up, you are layering and not multitasking. You are getting more than one thing done at a time, but once you hit "print" on the computer, press "clean" on the filter, and have dialed the parent's number you are getting more than one thing done at a time. However, you are **attentively focusing** only on filing papers. Layering also applies to grouping similar tasks or planning errands to the same location so that you don't lose time retrieving and putting away the same needed supplies or traveling around randomly each time you need something from the office. Layering applies to tasks that are mostly automatic (sharpening pencils, erasing the board, straightening desks, cutting out shapes, etc.) and don't need your conscious attention.

Rubenstein, Meyer, and Evans (2001) believe the simple reason that multitasking doesn't work is because we can't actually focus on more than one task at a time. But we think we can—so we multitask to try and get more done. Imagine trying to write an e-mail to a parent while mediating a dispute between two students. Both tasks involve communication. You cannot clearly focus on both tasks at the same time, so your mind gets overloaded as you switch between the two.

Another major downside to multitasking is the effect it has on our stress levels. Dealing with multiple things at once can cause the brain to produce adrenaline and other stress hormones that make us feel "on edge." Over time, the result of this overstimulation can leave us feeling overwhelmed, exhausted, and disoriented.

Suggestions for *Single-Tasking* at School

1. When you are with students, be fully present with them. Turn off personal e-mail, tweets, Instagrams, and texts. Limit *teacher drama* and save personal matters for another time. Try to leave your home life at home.

2. Clear your workstations of clutter. You don't have to be the King or Queen of Organization, but your life will be easier to manage if you can find the things you need.

3. Learn to delegate jobs to students. You don't have to feed the iguana, sell the cheerleader ribbons, focus the LCD projector, or even write your objectives on the board. Kids can be taught to do those and other tasks (and some of them love to do them).

4. Keep a running list of things to do later. You can capture random thoughts on your electronic device or on a pad of paper, but jotting things down allows you to move them out of your present thoughts and concentrate on the task at hand. (Just be sure to check your list at a designated later time.)

5. Try to finish one task before beginning another. The positive momentum of completing a job is energizing, and you will end up saving time. ∎

LEARN HOW AND WHEN TO SAY NO

How many of you educators are presently thinking, "I just don't have quite enough things to do in my life. I'm a little bored. How can I get my superiors to add one or two more things to my plate?" That would be *no teacher ever*. As a matter of fact, we believe that it should be a rule that no one can add another task to a teacher's assignments without removing something equally time consuming. Given that our time is already overcommitted and we are stretched as thin as we can stretch, many of us still lack the ability to say no when asked to handle even more responsibilities. Maybe because we see ourselves as helpers and caregivers, we feel compelled to step up and chair the Math-a-thon, edit the student newsletter, sponsor the pep squad, donate a tutoring session, and dozens of other worthy causes that present themselves each year. Many times we do it because it seems that no one else will do it, and we can't live with the guilt of not volunteering.

We (the authors) are all for volunteering. We think being willing to help others is part of our noble profession, and individuals ought to give their time, talent, and material assets to others when they choose to. The problem comes when we commit to more things than we can effectively do. It is so easy to say, "Yes, I'll help with that," when the task is 6 months away. (Always remember: Dates are closer than they appear on the calendar.) Then when the time is upon us, we lament, "Oh, I can't believe I let them talk me into doing this. I don't even have time to change my bulletin boards, let alone take care of this chore!" We think teachers should carefully select the causes and activities they most want to support and leave the rest to others. When we overcommit, we become "nonjoyful givers," and that defeats the whole purpose of giving, right? It also adds to our stress levels.

Have you ever noticed that no matter what the request made of faculty members, there are always one or two who never get pressured into volunteering nor seem to feel guilty about not stepping up? Do you secretly envy their ability to say no and get away with it? Do you sometimes wish you could be a little more assertive about not getting roped into things you wish you had not agreed to do? Perhaps it is time you learned the secret to avoiding being manipulated into overcommitting.

First of all, stop volunteering for things you cannot do, do not wish to do, or do not have the time or energy for. If you are asked directly to take on another responsibility you need to think about your personal well-being and the effect the added responsibility will take on your time and stress level. The art of saying no to a colleague or to an administrator begins with a little assertiveness training. You do not need to be aggressive, hostile, or rude, but you do need to mean what you say. Don't whine, hedge, or offer an apology.

> *Sometimes, "No" is an option. Don't be afraid to say "No." Parents, teachers, and students are often accustomed to being told "Yes," but when that is not a logical or ethical response, try saying "No."*
>
> —Jack Berckemeyer

 ## Scenario

In a faculty meeting, the administrator is trying to enlist volunteers for a special project. He spies you and pleads, "Theresa, I really need a sponsor for this year's Help-A-Child Foundation, and you are such a terrific organizer, I'd like to enlist your help. As you know, this event is an important part of our community's outreach to needy children, and of course, being a parent yourself, I know you'll want to contribute. Just look at these pictures I have of young children with sad little smudged faces. Doesn't it just break your heart? May I count on you to take over this year's fundraiser?"■

Normal responses are, "I'd like to help, but I don't have time." "Oh gee, I can't do it at this time." "Well, I'd like to help but . . ." None of these are what an assertive person says because they leave you open for arguments and more appeals. Don't allow any discussion on the issue, and don't say, "I can't do it this time," because it sounds like you are volunteering for next year.

In her workshops on teacher time management, Debbie Silver suggests that individuals give a 3-point response:

3-Point Response

In a calm but firm voice you say:

1. **"I appreciate the vote of confidence."** (In other words, stop blowing smoke up my dress; you're not going to flatter me into this.)

2. **"I think the Help-a-Child Foundation is a worthy cause, and I hope this year's event is a tremendous success."** (So quit showing me pictures of sad little kids, trying to manipulate me with sob stories, or otherwise selling me on the cause.)

3. **"For several reasons, I have to say no."** (Break eye contact—he who blinks, loses. Do not hedge, mumble, or whine. Clearly and succinctly turn down the offer, and shift your attention to other things—or better yet, walk away. Assertive people state their cases simply and quietly and offer no explanation or apology.)

Then most importantly, don't feel guilty or responsible. By not volunteering for everything that comes your way, you can often nudge others into roles they may need to try. You also save your time and attention for causes that are personally gratifying to you and, therefore, cause you less stress. Being a "nonjoyful giver" does not help you or the cause in the long run. Say no and mean it. Practice the 3-point response until you can do it without an apologetic voice, any additional explanation, or lingering guilt. Your time is one of your most precious commodities. Take control of it and invest it carefully. ■

YOU ARE WHAT YOU EAT

No one reading this chapter needs a lecture on healthy eating. Every educated person is regularly inundated with information about what constitutes wise decisions about food and beverage choices. Advertisers make sure we are aware of the latest and greatest food products that promote health and longevity. Knowing is not the problem. Choosing is the problem.

Rational human beings who drive cars put fuel in them so that they will run. Most of us are pretty selective about what kind of fuel we put in our vehicles. We know that higher grades may cost a little more but will be better for the auto in the long run. We realize that input generally equals performance. But when it comes to our bodies, we forget that food is supposed to be fuel that helps us perform at our best.

Skipping meals, eating low nutrient snacks, or indulging in food/drinks we know are detrimental to our short-term performance and/or long-term endurance is just not smart. And if we choose to make choices that are less than brainy, then the least we can do is take responsibility for our choices.

Let's say our infamous curmudgeon, Ms. Culsmucker, enters the lounge on a Monday morning griping and complaining because she woke up late, had bus duty, and had no chance to eat breakfast. She is cranky and upset because she knows she will have to spend lunch grading the papers she didn't get to last night, so she's already projecting what a horrid day it is going to be. Suddenly, she spies a huge cake purchased in honor of all faculty members with birthdays this month. She grabs a huge corner piece with extra icing, scarfs it down, and polishes it off with approximately half a liter of punch. Can you predict what she is going to be like in about 15 minutes when all that sugar hits her system? She is going to be like a mosquito on speed. Before first period is over, she will write 15 referrals, chew out her aide, and dash off a vile e-mail to all the parents blaming them for procreating in the first place. And, of course, by the time her afternoon classes are scheduled to begin, she will be barely able to put one foot in front of the other. She will blame all her woes on the students, their parents, her colleagues, her administrators, the school, and anyone but herself. Maybe it is time for a chat about personal responsibility.

We believe that teachers should be aware of their personal body needs and take care of them. Whether you are someone who thrives on the largely carbohydrate fare served in the lunchroom or one who needs several small protein-rich snacks spread out throughout the day, make it happen. As far as we know, teachers are not required to eat what others prepare. If you have lunchroom duty, you can still take your own food with you. If you need to keep fruit or a protein snack cold, put a refrigerator in your room. (Yes, we know some schools do not allow that. So, get one and hide it . . . or . . . bring a small ice chest, carry an insulated lunch bag, or make friends with the human ecology teacher and use her fridge.) The point is, take care of yourself.

Many schools now offer wellness programs for their teachers. Even if you're not lucky enough to have such a program, you can usually find a colleague who shares your interest in good nutrition and can swap turns bringing healthy snacks, remind you about your goals, and encourage you when it's definitely a Need-for-Chocolate Day. It isn't so much about losing weight to look better as it is about being the weight you need to be in order to do your personal best. Forget about the scale, pant size, or the mirror; just decide to make it part of your daily routine to eat foods that are right for you and limit those that are not. It takes lots of energy to be an effective teacher, and optimism is fueled by food as well as the soul.

STAY HYDRATED

Readers are aware of the research on drinking plenty of water throughout the day. Although we are big proponents of drinking pure water (easier on the bladder and kidneys), the main idea is to take in enough fluids of any kind to keep the body hydrated. Juice, sodas, coffee, tea, energy drinks, and even some foods count toward getting enough fluid. (And as teachers we all know, "caffeine is our friend.")

A mere 2 percent drop in body fluids can lead to inability to focus on a computer screen, trouble with concentration, and fuzzy math (we thought we were bad at arithmetic, but now we know we were just thirsty). Dehydration is the number one cause of afternoon fatigue, and bodies can become dehydrated long before we feel thirst. Both educators and their students need to drink plenty of fluids throughout the school day to remain mentally alert and at their physical best. The bottom line is this: If you want to stay positive and joyful, you have to take good care of yourself. Eat right and drink plenty of fluids (preferably pure water). No surprise there.

EXERCISE—"I CAN'T RUN BECAUSE I'LL SPILL MY DRINK."

Not only is it recommended that humans get regular cardiovascular exercise (aerobics, running, swimming, etc.), but as we age, we are advised to include regular strength and anaerobic workouts. Doctors tell us that nearly every medical condition and ailment can be improved with regular exercise. That includes cancer, diabetes, heart problems, arthritis, immune deficiencies, common colds, joint pain, insomnia, high blood pressure, dementia, depression, and more. Exercise is one of the simplest and most direct ways to improve our attitudes as well as our physical health. So why do people avoid it?

For many of us, the thought of exercise conjures up all kinds of painful memories (literally and figuratively). We see our more athletic friends wearing their "I Run for Life" t-shirts as we proudly brandish our "I Run for No One" stretchy sweats. We snarl, "It's all about genetics, and my genes are just fluffy," as we avoid all exercise except pulling up the lever on our recliners.

There is not time or space here to address all the excuses many of us use for not exercising. You may hear yourself saying, "Oh no, I missed going to the gym today . . . that makes 5 years in a row." But we are all more than aware it is impossible to think about taking care of ourselves without considering a regular, sustainable exercise plan.

Again, many schools offer exercise sessions, weight room availability, and innovative programs such as *zumba* and *jazzercise* for their teachers. Whether our school does or does not offer wellness opportunities, it is up to us as individuals to take responsibility for taking care of our bodies. Our wonderful spirits won't survive long without a suitable place to reside.

Many times people think that to start exercising means to jump in and "go for the gold." That's only if you want to be sure you won't keep it up. Instead of "going for the gold," we believe you should go for the beige or pink or chartreuse or whatever represents one step ahead of where you are now. Start small. Take the stairs more times that you have to. Practice holding in your stomach as tightly as you can between classes. Walk around your classroom constantly instead of standing, sitting, or propping yourself against something. Bend over from the waist to retrieve items (real or imaginary) from the floor. Stretch every chance you get.

And here's the good news. You don't have to run or do calisthenics if you don't want to. You don't have to get on a treadmill or join an aerobics class if that's not your preference. You just have to do something—anything. You can do yourself just as much good with regular fast-paced walking through your neighborhood as running around a track. You can dance yourself into fitness, skate yourself into better shape, or play certain sports to get into good condition. It's really a matter of figuring out what you find most appealing and doing it regularly. We all need to remember that our energy, our optimism, and our health are influenced by the choices we make. It is an individual responsibility.

SLEEP IS NOT JUST FOR SLACKERS

Experts recommend 7 to 8 hours of sleep for most every night (Van Dongen, Maisliln, Mullington, & Dinges, 2003, p. 125). Teachers often chuckle when we tell them that. They protest that they can't do all they need to do in their lives if they sleep that much. They tell us that in order to make a living, they need to be awake for at least 19–20 hours a day. Our answer is simple—you probably won't be living much longer if you keep that up.

Sometimes people equate the need for sleep with some sort of weakness, an indicator of laziness, or just an excuse to get out of doing things. That's indeed unfortunate because people who go without regular restorative sleep are asking for all kinds of mental and health problems. Studies have documented the negative effect of sleep deprivation on memory, reaction time, comprehension, and attention. Even physical and emotional states can be affected. Scientists are attributing an increasing amount of health issues to the lack of quality sleep. Altered levels of hormones resulting from poor sleep patterns can affect metabolism, weight, mood, and cardiovascular health. More recently scientists have associated sleep deprivation with the body's immune system, thus pointing to the importance of sleep in fighting immune disorders, including cancer. Additionally, neuroscientists have linked sleep to learning and memory. Proper sleep is essential to physical, mental, and emotional health (Bryant, 2008).

According to sleep researchers, a night's sleep is divided into five continually shifting stages, defined by types of brain waves that reflect either lighter or deeper sleep. Toward morning, there is an increase in rapid eye movement, or REM sleep, when the muscles are relaxed and dreaming occurs, and recent memories may be consolidated in the brain. The experts say that hitting a snooze alarm over and over again to wake up is not the best way to feel rested because this on-and-off-again effect of dozing and waking causes shifts in the brainwave patterns and impairs their mental functioning during the day (Heaner, 2004).

There is also the conundrum that stress can cause people to lose sleep, and sleep loss can cause stress. Many times, though, the sleep disorder starts with a physiological reason. More and more teachers tell us that either they or their significant other snores loudly or suffers from the much more serious condition of sleep apnea. Since one of the authors has had sleep apnea for over 20 years, we are quite familiar with its ramifications. It is a destructive and sometimes deadly condition in which during sleep, a person stops breathing for as long as a minute and then gasps desperately for air. This happens over and over during the sleep cycle, but the apnea sufferer never fully wakes up or fully gets REM sleep. It disrupts the sleep of not only the sufferer but also of anyone within earshot of the snorting, gasping person with the apnea.

> *Getting enough sleep, feeling rested, and being healthy: Generally, bad days happen when I'm feeling tired, run-down, or sick. I've found that they're less like to occur if I'm regularly getting my exercise (which has been playing basketball at a mediocre skill level for 40 years).*
>
> —Larry Ferlazzo, teacher, author, *Education Week Teacher* blogger

We recommend that anyone who has or suspects she has a sleep disorder should schedule an appointment with an ear, nose, and throat specialist, a neurologist, or a specialized sleep doctor. If the problem is with the person sharing your bedroom, we advise you to encourage him to at least have the condition checked out. You may want to point out to him that sleep apnea restricts oxygen intake and can permanently enlarge his heart. It also leads to other heart problems, strokes, and all manner of ill effects. Look it up and see how serious a health problem it is.

Our bodies have extraordinary ways of telling us when they need to rest, restore, and rejuvenate. Sleep is not a luxury, nor is it self-indulgent. It is a vital part of keeping ourselves fully functioning and ready to be deliberately optimistic. If you are tired, rest. If you are sleepy, go to sleep. Be creative and find a way to get in a nap or go to bed at a reasonable time.

OTHER WAYS TO TAKE CARE OF YOURSELF

Probably we could write an entire book just on the topic of taking care of ourselves as teachers. Not only do we need to be at our personal best for ourselves, but we are role models for young people and often an inspiration to folks we don't even know about. Everyone knows the basics—eat right, get plenty of rest, exercise, and drink enough water. We have just a few more we'd like you to consider because we think you are worth it. (See the Appendix, page 156, for a summary list of 12 ways to reduce stress.)

1. Make sure you have a "go to" person. In Chapter 4, we discuss the importance of building relationships with colleagues. Hopefully there is someone at your school who is your *safety net*, someone who will stand by you no matter what. If you don't have that person at your school, try to cultivate a friendship with someone within at least an hour's drive from you who would come and help you no matter the time of day or night. How do you find somebody like that? As your mother always told you, "The best way to have that kind of friend is to be that kind of friend."

 ## Definition of a Friend

A **real friend** will come and help you if you call no matter what the time of day or night.

A **better friend** will come and help you move.

A **"Go-To" friend** will come and help you move bodies—no questions asked. ■

2. Be proactive: Get annual check-ups. Regularly see your physician, your optometrist, your dentist, your dermatologist, and any specialist you need to see. Pap smears, mammograms, colonoscopies, skin biopsies, and other regular tests can save your life or certainly improve the quality of it. Like us, you probably can name some important people in your circle who are gone too soon simply because they failed to get the kinds of tests and information they needed in a timely manner. If you can't make time for the tests, how are you going to make time for the surgeries and treatments you will need because you didn't get tested?

3. Try to relax during some part of each day. We are not recommending that you have Sven, the masseuse, pop in to give you a back massage during your unruly sixth-hour class, but we do think it's imperative that educators find some way to break the tension of the rigorous work we do at least sometime during each day. Whether it is isolating yourself in a restroom stall, hiding out in the book stacks in the media center, or even just sitting in your car in the parking lot, it is important to find some alone time to decompress and breathe. Deep breaths are calming. You can also read something inspirational, listen to soothing music, write in your journal, or just sit quietly and gather your thoughts.

The cover of *Time Magazine* on February 3, 2014, introduces the topic of the *mindfulness revolution*. Mindfulness is a kind of secular meditation that helps people become fully aware of themselves and their surroundings. Its popularity is increasing, and it is being taught in many schools to help students regulate their behavior and focus their attention. Schools across the country are embracing the concept of short, quiet, attentive periods during the school day to help both teachers and students fully relax and refresh themselves for further learning. Whether or not there is a mindfulness program at your school, you can learn to meditate or reflect for a short time during the day to renew your spirit and enhance your state of mind.

4. If you need help, see an expert. Educators are some of the worst procrastinators when it comes to seeking help for mental distress. Maybe it's because we've all taken classes in psychology or human behavior and consider ourselves to be experts in the field. Or maybe it's because we're so busy helping everybody else with their problems that we feel there's no time to concentrate on our own. Or perhaps we've just bought into that *Superman/Wonder Woman Teacher* image that makes us think we just need to *tough things out.*

Whatever the reason, it is ridiculous to think we can solve our own mental anguish by ourselves. Just as we counsel others to get help from experts, so should we. When we are clinically depressed, emotionally frazzled, or dealing with serious issues, it is important to remember that our friends and family may want to help us, but they can't. We need an unbiased third party to give us perspective and to listen without judgment. It is essential to seek out a counselor, theologian, psychologist, psychiatrist, or other trained mental health professional. Some even offer fees on a sliding scale, so cost doesn't have to be an issue.

Most of us have times in our lives when we need to hear the viewpoint of someone trained to deal with mental pain. Don't say to yourself, "This is ridiculous. I know a lot about mental health, and knowing what I know, I should be able to take care of this by myself." Instead please say, "I am going through a tough time right now, and I could use the help of someone trained to deal with this kind of situation. This is the best investment of my time and money I can make right now. I am going to do this because I am worth it." Then do it. Sometimes the greatest demonstration of optimism is being able to reach out when you need help.

Simple steps, right? Most of you are nodding your heads and saying, "Yes, I know I need to work on . . ." Whatever it is that goes in the next part of that sentence for you, please do it. Kids are counting on you. And you are so worth it!

Action Steps for Teachers

DISCUSSION QUESTIONS AND ACTIVITIES

1. Try your hand at writing your own "Top 10 Ways You Know You Are an Educator Under Too Much Stress." Be as funny and creative as you can. If you don't mind sharing, please forward your list (along with names and schools of the writers) to debbie@debbiesilver.com. We promise to mention you in any ideas we "borrow" for future publications.

2. Describe how your body lets you know when you are under too much stress. What do you do when that happens? Why?

3. Explain any recent research you have read about multitasking. Do you agree that multitasking on anything except noncognitive tasks is impossible? Why or why not?

4. Describe a situation in which you were multitasking to the nth degree. How did you feel while it was going on? How effectively did you complete each task? Do you think that you saved time in the long run by doing more than one thing at a time? Why or why not?

5. Make an argument for teachers *single-tasking* when students are present in the classroom. Make an argument for *layering* when students are present in the classroom.

6. When asked to *volunteer* for extra assignments and work you don't want to do, what is the benefit of using the Debbie Silver's 3-Point Response? How is that preferable to the answer, "I'm just too busy right now to take on another thing. Are you going to be mad at me if I say no?"

7. Would you recommend your present dietary habits to your students? Why or why not?

8. What reasonable modifications to your present exercise program could you make now that would greatly enhance your fitness by this time next year? Do you think you will make the change(s) you just listed? Why or why not?

9. Identify your normal sleep habits and defend their appropriateness for your long-term health goals.

10. List at least five things you do every week just to take care of you. What is your rationale behind doing those things?

Action Steps for School Leaders

1. Arrange for a local masseuse or two to come to school for a day and do chair massages. Staff members can sign up for 10- to 15-minute intervals throughout the day. Don't forget to get one yourself.

2. Set up a health fair just for staff members at your school. Have medical people on hand to do blood tests, cholesterol checks, eye screens, and whatever else you think would be helpful to your staff. Also invite dieticians, exercise pros, and other people who work with wellness to set up tables and offer free advice and brochures.

3. Invite a sleep expert to present to your faculty about the importance of sleep for them and for the students they teach.

4. Investigate getting discount memberships for all staff members to a local health club or exercise facility.

5. Invest in putting a couple of treadmills in the teacher lounge. Sometimes walking helps re-energize people (and fast walking may be a healthy outlet for a teacher who is just about ready to snap).

6. Employ good-spirited humor to encourage positive communication and to ease tense situations. Encourage staff members to do the same. Smiling and good-natured laughter are two indicators of a healthy school climate.

7. Encourage staff to dress professionally but give them permission to wear comfortable shoes—even athletic shoes. Nothing is so tiring as standing in dressy, uncomfortable shoes all day.

8. Do everything you can to accommodate a teacher's request for adjusting the temperature in her room. Telling her "There's no way you can be hot" doesn't help. An exceedingly uncomfortable room temperature (hot or cold) can be highly stressful.

9. At the beginning of the year, ask staff members to write down the name of their all-time favorite nonalcoholic drink. At stressful times during the year surprise them by having their selections delivered to their classrooms. (You don't have to do them all on the same day, but make sure you eventually get around to everyone.)

10. When you are aware that a teacher is having a particularly stressful time, volunteer to either assist with his class or take over his class while he does what he needs to do to get himself together. When he thanks you, simply tell him, "It was my pleasure. You're worth it." And never mention it again.

CHAPTER 8

Joyful School Communities

The Sum of Their Parts

When we become a really mature, grown-up, wise society, we will put teachers at the center of the community, where they belong. We don't honor them enough, we don't pay them enough.

—Charles Kuralt, Academy of Achievement
Archives, Washington, DC

Most of what we have written so far in this book focuses on what we as educators can do for ourselves to reclaim our joy in and our hopefulness for the teaching profession. We want to also take a look at what administrators, parents, and local communities can do to help restore optimism and hope in our nation's schools, and of course, what teachers can do beyond their own classrooms.

Andy Hargreaves and Michael Fullan (2013) write about increasing *professional capital* to improve education in the United States. They are referring to a practice of elevating the teaching profession across the board with higher pay, more autonomy, more trust, more time for professional development, and more attention to retaining an experienced, excellent workforce. They state that countries like Finland, Singapore, and Canada develop the whole profession rather than focusing on removing the few at the bottom or rewarding only those at the top. Hargreaves and Fullan maintain that government bodies need to demonstrate courage and faith in investing in teacher development and empowerment.

To attract people to the profession, you need a good set of schools for those people to work in. Continuous professional development pays off in Finland, Singapore, Alberta, and Ontario. The best way you can support and motivate teachers is to create the conditions where they can be effective day after day, together. And this isn't just about intraschool collaboration. It's about interschool and interdistrict collaboration. It's about the whole profession. (p. 37)

It is good to read comments from people like the late Charles Kuralt, social commentator, as well as respected researchers Andy Hargreaves and Michael Fullan, who agree the teaching profession needs a new appreciation and perhaps a new focus. We could not agree more. We would add that we think schools need to follow other top educational countries in providing teachers with unencumbered time during the school day to study, collaborate, and reflect on their practices. One reason U.S. teachers feel so on edge is that there is little or no time in their school day schedule for professional deliberations or personal growth.

However, this book is written to address Five Principles of Deliberate Optimism, and one of those principles is to **focus on what individual teachers, administrators, and schools can actually *do*** now to retain our hopeful attitudes and contribute to a more optimistic presence in education.

Educators must, now more than ever, be prepared to step up and take a more forceful stand in promoting what they believe constitutes a quality education. They can no longer cede to politicians and business leaders the task of determining the purpose of an education, and then dictating it to educators, students, and the general public.

—Michael R. Connolly, Jr., educator, author (2013)

THE ADMINISTRATORS

Rafe Esquith (2014) believes that

School morale begins at the top, and when school leaders respect and believe in their teachers, everyone wins. Most staff members are more than willing to do some of the more unpleasant parts of their jobs because they work for a principal who rolls up his sleeves and works alongside them. (p. 21)

Most teachers reading this chapter are now shouting, "Amen! Yes, that's what *They* should be doing." But let's be fair and make sure teachers do what they can to support administrators. School leaders are busy people. Whereas we have to answer to our students and their families, the administrator has many more constituents to connect with, including the teachers, the staff, all of the families, the district officials, the school board, the broader community, and the secretary who runs the front office. Today's school principals and their assistants have truckloads of paperwork, endless meetings, and constantly evolving demands. Many administrators

Dina Strasser (2014) interviewed principals and teachers in New York's Rochester City School District to ask about how administrators can help build and sustain teacher morale. Collectively, they came up with some interesting, but probably not surprising, advice for administrators:

1. First have the common courtesy to give teachers what they ask for. If a teacher asks to have a refrigerator in her room, why make her defend her reason? Why not just get one for her? When teachers say they need more paper, more books, or more science supplies, why not trust that they know what it takes to get the job done and move heaven and earth to make sure they have what they need? If the request is impossible, why not work on a suitable alternative with the teacher?

2. Communication cannot be emphasized strongly enough. Ironically, some of the world's worst communicators see themselves as extremely proficient in that area. Start by either you and/or your assistant routinely popping in and out of classes as part of the culture (rather than "I gotcha!"). Be honest with teachers. If the district has told you to check that everyone's learning goals are on the board, be transparent and tell them, "Today I'll be dropping into everyone's rooms to check that your learning goals are written in the top right-hand corner of your board. Not my idea, by the way." Tell teachers as openly as you can about the complexities of running the school.

Make it a point to know about staff members' situations, families, and other important personal data.

3. Treat teachers like adults. Give teachers autonomy and do not try to micromanage their lesson plans, e-mails, sick leave, or departure time from school. Involve them in planning their schedules and be flexible with them about attending to their own family needs. Work on the premise that as long as the work gets done, essential ideas are taught, and connections are made with kids and their families, teachers can have the flexibility to determine how they spend their time.

4. Play with the *gray area*. There is sometimes a tension between doing what the district wants and what is morally and ethically correct for teachers; err to the side of the teachers. Fight for your teachers, and let them know you are doing just that.

5. Remember that morale is only a side effect. A former school superintendent wrote, "Teacher morale, in my experience, is not a function of practices designed to maintain or create it. It is a by-product of being treated as leaders and being treated with respect. Teacher morale is the end product of empowering teachers to make decisions that affect their lives."

SOURCE: Strasser (2014). Adapted from "An Open Letter on Teacher Morale," by Dina Strasser, in the February 2014 issue of *Educational Leadership* (71) 5, pp. 10-13. © 2014 by ASCD. Used with permission. Learn more about ASCD at www.ascd.org.

would love to be with the students, would enjoy tossing around ideas on how to make the school a joyful environment, but they just don't see where they have the time.

Their minimal resource of extra time is why ideas about the actions we wish to take toward building a positive school climate should be well thought out and involve as little effort on the part of the administrators as possible. It won't work to say "*You* should . . ." or "Why don't *you* . . . ?" Instead, we need to prepare our plans beforehand and let the administrator know we will take the lead to do what needs to be done. We are just meeting with him or her to provide the necessary information and ensure it works with his or her school plan.

Ascribing it to many factors, teachers often admit they spend little time talking educational philosophy with peers. It is even more rare for teachers and administrators to spend time conversing philosophically about real educational issues. Opening day speeches and faculty meetings are filled with data and detritus (much of which could be better communicated electronically). While some schools encourage teams to discuss books or articles together as part of their professional development, the administrators often have only enough time to sit briefly with a team before moving on to some crisis. We need to try and find a way to help our administrator(s) carve out some time to discuss our shared overall school belief systems.

Remember, too, that administrators' lives are relatively lonely in regard to their connection with school. We have our teammates and students to engage us each day—the administrators often have little else but problems and paperwork. Perhaps we teachers could occasionally send a little note of affirmation, a birthday/holiday remembrance, a random flower or treat on the desk, or a thank-you for a specific deed. Everyone likes to be valued, and sometimes school leaders get left out of the mix. Remember they are often caught in the middle. Everything from the district runs downhill to their desks, and everything at the school runs uphill to the same place. It's not usually a fun place to be.

And for goodness sake, we need to avoid the *talking snake* in the lounge who criticizes every move the administrator makes. Or maybe we need to go into the lounge and stick up for the person not there to defend himself or herself. Often these diatribes are founded on rumor or guilt (many of them are just worried that someone will find out how poorly they do their own jobs and are trying to put the focus on anyone but themselves).

When controversial issues come to light, go straight to the administrator to get the facts. Principle one of deliberate optimism—**gather as much information about the situation as possible**. But be aware that a lot of what weighs heavily on the minds of administrators is information they cannot share with others, even in defense of themselves. They are privy to all kinds of private data about the central office, personnel, students, the parents, and more information than they want to know. They are obliged by professionalism not to discuss these matters, and perhaps we should be a little more tolerant about giving them the benefit of the doubt.

If, by chance, you have an administrator who is not really suited to run a joyful school, do what you can to work with and around him or her. This can usually be done without calling attention to the individual's deficits. Stick to the idea of planning ahead in order to make it easier for the administrator to say yes, because there is little he or she is required to do to make your plan work. Support what you can. Be positive. Use the strength of your caucus (discussed later in this chapter). Bring along chocolate.

The Parents

We hope it does not surprise you to learn that the families of your students also want your school to be a warm, caring, and positive environment. The 2013 Gallup Poll on Education found that the adults surveyed thought teachers today should be more caring and interested. Now before you get furious, reflect on all that we have said so far in this book. Perhaps you are reading this alone. Perhaps you are sharing it with your team or book group. Are you sharing it with the families of the children who attend your school? How can they know about what's bugging us or what's encouraging you, if we don't tell them? Who tells them about the novel ideas you have or strategies you think will change your classroom or school into a new creation? How do they know about the countless hours you spend enhancing your skills and building your knowledge base? If we don't tell them, who will?

> *You can never help a student by alienating his parents.*
>
> —Debbie Silver

Let's first deal with the families of the students you teach. You probably spend a lot of time connecting with parents—via classroom/team newsletter, e-mail blasts, parent portal information, etc. If you are aware that not all of your parents have computer access at home, you likely also use paper communication, phone calls, etc. Most teachers today believe they are communicating a lot of information all the time, and they are. On the other hand, it is evident that the connection is mostly one-way. Oh sure, you were wise enough to send out a sheet before school began, asking parents to comment on their child's strengths and weaknesses, hopes and dreams, but then what? What is missing is not *communication*, it's *conversation*. Conversation is two-sided, give-and-take, and alas, time-consuming. But if you have friends, lovers, or a medical problem, you cannot deny the urgency and fruitfulness of a two-sided conversation. And this is often what is missing for us as educators when it comes to connecting with parents. We pour information out over them like a reservoir spillway and generally miss seeing them sputter and gurgle with the flow. One 10- or 15-minute conversation can make all the difference, especially for families who aren't used to navigating a large—or even small—school system.

When and where do we have these conversations? Let's start with open house or return to school night. Make it a point to have two or three actual conversations that night. Use questions such as "What are you most concerned about this year?" "What is your child most looking forward to?" "Is there something I can do to make this year more fun/challenging/interesting for your child?" They will remember that you listened to them and appreciate you for it. Make a note of the parents/guardians with whom you speak as the year progresses so that you can make sure you don't leave anyone out.

You might try to have three telephone or Skype conversations each week with different families. You could have a brief conversation with the parent/guardian volunteering in the school or on the playground. Conversations can take place in the basketball stands or during carpool. These conversations build relationships essential to forming the basis for a joyful parental community.

Besides having ongoing communication and conversations with parents, educators should consider involving parents in the school day in ways other than supervising lunch or supervising the field trip. While these efforts are wonderful ways of engaging parents and guardians in their child's school, they are not available opportunities for everyone. As part of building relationships with students and their families, find out what work the parent or guardian does. It doesn't matter what the job is—students are interested in the adult world of work and would love to hear a brief presentation on any parent's job. Also, some parents have skills at sewing, designing, inventing, experimenting, showing, and/or teaching that students appreciate. Invite those parents into your classroom. Once you have them there, you can build a relationship that will serve you well as you work with them to ensure the success of their children.

Many teachers realize the value of the assignment notebook or planner as a tool for communication. If students are required to write in their planner a sentence summarizing what happened in class, they not only have a memory-jog as they start their homework, but they also have information for a parent perusing the planner. We all know that young people can be totally noncommunicative when it comes to talking about school, particularly as they advance in grade levels. A vague question such as, "What'd you do in school today?" is generally met by, "Nothing," or "Why?" (Or, if they remember, "Bob threw up.") Planners help parents ask more direct questions: "It says here you saw a movie in science, what was it about?" "What did your teacher say today about the Civil Rights Movement?" "When is this Spanish skit due?"

The important thing to remember is that our lives and the lives of our students are better served if we can involve their parents in positive relationships. It's hard to dislike someone who genuinely likes your child, so perhaps we need to do a better job of communicating what it is we do like about our students to their parents.

Building the relationships with honest, affirming comments about their offspring goes a long way to helping parents listen when we have to offer news that is not so great or advice that is hard to hear. Both types of communication are sometimes necessary in working for the benefit of the student.

A dynamic opportunity for having a conversation and/or building relationships is the parent conference. Student-led conferences (SLCs) are undoubtedly one of the most successful educational strategies available, but they should not take the place of conversations between teachers and parents. Conversations with parents reinforce both parties' concern for the student and a mutual willingness to act as resources going forward.

Involving parents in our goal to provide a challenging, engaging, caring, safe environment for students only makes sense. They are a huge part of the success equation for their kids, and they are an integral part of how joyful our teaching experience is. Several of the ideas for relationship building in Chapters 3 and 4 can also be applied to parents and guardians.

STUDENT-LED CONFERENCES: BUILDING A CULTURE OF RELATIONSHIP, COMMUNICATION, AND ACCOUNTABILITY

While we definitely want teachers to have significant conversations with the parents, we also think it is our job to help parents have meaningful conversations with their offspring. SLCs force students to set their own goals and outline their plans to meet those goals.

SLCs are something that all grade levels, PreK–12, and schools should seriously consider. They help build a better relationship between teachers and students and between students and parents. They give more ownership and more responsibility to the student and give them an opportunity to have a voice and choice in their education.

STUDENT-LED CONFERENCE OVERVIEW

Students as young as kindergarten participate in SLCs all around the United States. Each age level can show progress in learning and share information about what material has been mastered, what still needs work. Students can use paper or electronic portfolios. SLCs hold very little resemblance to traditional parent-teacher conferences. Let parents and students know well in advance about the change in format.

The goal is to have the student lead the conference, show his or her work, answer questions, set goals and provide a tentative action plan. It is important that both parents and students be prepared for SLCs.

- Student preparation includes selecting three or four examples that show work accomplished, progress made, hurdles to overcome; writing a script (detailed or loose, depending on the student's age and confidence level); and practicing their presentations in front of another student.

- Parent preparation includes their receiving a clear description of how the conference will work; formulating two or three guiding questions to ask during the conference; and understanding the demand that the conference be completely positive.

- Sometimes a demonstration of a classroom activity is useful to assist parents in understanding the work.

Teachers Note: Let the student lead the conference. You are there simply to facilitate the student's presentation and ensure that the student's work is honored. Be clear that behavioral or social issues or other parental concerns should be discussed at another time. Do not show grades until the very end of the meeting.

- After the conferences are completed, have students send thank-you notes to their parents for attending. This note might also review the goals and action plan offered at the conference (e.g., "I agreed to check over my work before I turned it in, to devote an extra 10 minutes every day to reading, and to make sure I turn my work in on the day assigned").

As you can see, this is merely an overview. We would encourage you as an individual teacher or team of teachers to use the principles of optimism to plan for SLCs. SLCs can have a huge impact for you as the educator and for your students. For more resources and a readiness quiz, see "Student-Led Conferences" in the Appendix, page 157.

THE COMMUNITY: "IT TAKES A VILLAGE"

Okay, we're a little tired of that "takes a village" slogan, too, but there is a certain truth to it. Successful schools can help build positive communities, and likewise, healthy, thriving communities can help influence positive schools. Even though parents and guardians are part of the larger community in which your school functions, statistically, it is likely that fewer than 30 percent of the households in your community have a child in school. As a result, most the adults in your area have no clue what is happening there.

The same Gallup Poll we mentioned earlier showed (as it has every year the poll has been taken) that most parents/guardians give their child's school a "B" rating. **More than two thirds of parents are okay with what's happening in their child's school.** Why then, does education get such a bad reputation? One reason is the media portrays schools as dangerous and ineffective. In other words, the families of the students you teach are generally satisfied with what is happening at your school—it's *those other schools* that are in trouble. For community members who have no children in school, you are *those other schools*. A second reason teachers and education are misunderstood is that the public doesn't know what is happening in schools these days, and we don't take time to tell them.

Where does your general community, most of whom do not have children in school, get their information? For majority of them, they have to rely on the local media. We are all aware that newspapers and television are supported by advertising, and that the more the paper is read or the TV watched, the more ads are sold. It would seem that bad news sells more than good news, because media outlets certainly print or show more of the startling, bizarre, unsavory, murderous, and fantastic than they do the warm, humorous (except at someone's expense), generous, and caring. In other words, school shootings and bullying make better news than students happily engaging in everyday reading, writing, and all kinds of great learning activities. Local newspapers, however, are generally advocates of area schools and are interested in printing favorable coverage about their events and accomplishments. Savvy educators cultivate positive relationships with local reporters and regularly send them news stories to help inform the public about quality things going on in their schools.

Many adults not involved in education believe that schools aren't doing their job anymore. They have been told that schools do not teach handwriting or the right kind of math. They think teachers don't care. They think students are not being prepared as well as students in other countries. All of this habitual skepticism results in a strong opposing force that works against our movement toward optimism.

So perhaps it is time for us as teachers to educate the public about what is happening in our schools. See if you can find out how much your district spends on advertising and/or public relations each year. Most school districts spend nothing or next to nothing because they don't have to advertise to get kids to come to their school. It's a state requirement. But district administrators forget that a considerable number of taxpayers in their district have no idea what is happening in their local schools. Superintendents often don't focus on this disconnect until it is time to pass a bond issue or levy.

In her presentation, "Three C's for Parent Engagement," Judith Baenen offers these ideas:

1. If there is a bank within your district boundaries, go visit with the bank manager. The higher up in position in the bank (it'd be great if you could visit with the president) the better. Many banks have a requirement or at least a desire to serve the needs of the community in some way. They can help the school (no cost involved) by allowing you to display schoolwork in the lobby. You will assure them it will be attractive and appropriate. Then go back to school and add protective covers and borders to everyday work, lab reports, math assignments, social studies homework, etc., and arrange an exhibit for the bank lobby. Everyday work is the key—too often schools exhibit artwork or special poetry units. The ordinary tax-payer wants to see "schoolwork." When they enter the lobby of the bank, they will say things like, "Gee—this math looks hard. Wow, look what they're doing in sixth grade over at Lincoln School," or "Hmm, I didn't think they taught cursive writing anymore—look at this from Carver Elementary."

The bank can also occasionally allow you to use their electronic sign to adver-tise school successes like: ""Our whole eighth grade read *Diary of Anne Frank* last month" or "Our third graders have all mastered their multiplication timed test" or "Be sure to ask our tenth graders about their community service projects." Of course, if you have a band concert coming up, that can go there, too.

2. Another way of letting your community know what you are doing is to use your local eatery as a base for *advertising*. Here's how it works: You go to a nearby café or fast-food restaurant that uses placemats as part of the dining experience. It can be a chain or a local establishment. Talk to the manager. Offer to provide placemats for the restaurant for perhaps once each month. The advantage for the restaurant is that your placemats will increase the number of customers and also be good for the local school (win-win, wouldn't you say?). Back at school, laminate students' everyday schoolwork to approximate placemat size. Be sure to put the name of the school someplace on the mat. Inform parents that their child's work will be displayed at the local eatery (parents may have to provide permission).

Families whose children's work is on a placemat will visit the eatery to see and be proud and perhaps invite aunts, uncles, cousins, and neighbors, thereby increasing customers. Other customers will be exposed to everyday scholarship from your school. This idea can also be used for laminating or screening student work onto grocery bags for use at the nearby supermarket or store.

3. Of course, students are the best representatives of the school and offer a remarkable reality to taxpayers who believe all the negativity they read and hear from the media. Go to your local mall, shopping area, or grocery store. For this project, you need a long table, three to four students and an adult to supervise. This activity can be done once a month or more—check with the manager.

Take the students, the table, and the supervisor to the desired location and set up the table in a well-trafficked area. Have the students bring their everyday work. Give them a bit of training about how to speak with adults. The supervisor hangs back. When shoppers come by, the role of the student is to say, "Excuse me, ma'am. I'm from Lincoln School. Do you have a moment? I'd like to tell you what we're doing right now in math (science, social studies, technology, language arts, etc.)." The student then goes on to explain whatever is on his or her paper—any of which will likely blow the mind of the shopper. Later, that shopper will remember the child's politeness and intelligence—a credit to the school.

There are many ways to connect to the community, and perhaps you have tried many or all of these. You can partner with local businesses, you can invite in speakers, you can engage students in civic activities and clean-up projects. Keep at it—all of these activities enhance the joyfulness and optimism in the broader neighborhood in which you live. Often you will find support where you thought there was none, and you can bring that affirmation back to your classroom and shower it on the students.

TAKE BACK YOUR POWER

As we have said over and over in this book, it is time for us teachers to take back our power. The important thing to remember in all of this is that you are not in it alone. By careful listening, keeping an open attitude, and doing a little Nancy-Drew-like sleuthing, you can discover others on your team and in your building who want the same things for the students and the school that you do. There are teachers, support staff, and administrators who are working for the same goals. Additionally, the families of the students you teach provide wide avenues of support. Indeed, the community at large understands that a thriving local school is in everyone's best interest.

Maybe this means that you have to become a bit "political." Once you discover (through hearsay or obvious action) other teachers who share your attitude toward school and education, approach them openly to form an informal caucus. This caucus can

> ### Something to Work Toward
>
> *All teachers, especially newer teachers, should teach no more than four hours a day and spend the other four hours a day on their own learning and in collaboration with colleagues. They might study data about student learning and develop strategies for how to respond, observe in a master teacher's classroom, or write lesson plans and common assessments. They might coach other teachers, write curriculum, do policy work, and lead professional development.*
>
> —Joan Richardson, Editor-in-Chief, *Kappan* (2013)

    a. Tactfully share ideas with the school teams and administration

    b. Take action to implement the ideas

    c. Build a network to find other like-minded individuals

    d. Speak up about larger issues affecting educators and students

    e. Provide a support system when we inevitably stumble or miscue

Your caucus will attract both positive and negative attention, but that's fine. We need to get things out in the open and commence the candid discussions. In doing that, you will find other colleagues who will become part of your action. At least you will be **doing something toward your goal**, and that is one of the steps in the Principles of Deliberate Optimism. "Well okay, then. Get going!"

TELLING OUR STORIES

A vast majority of our power is the track record of what we have already done for our students. There are few veteran teachers who cannot recall at least one student's life they significantly changed. For most of us the list of lives we have impacted in a positive way would be quite lengthy.

And yet when is the last time you went into a teacher's lounge and heard someone say, "I think I changed a life today," "I think I made a difference," or even "I just ran into a young lady I taught 12 years ago, and you know what she said?"

In the fall of 2013, in order to support the United Way of Greater Toledo, Dr. Romules Durant, superintendent of Toledo Public Schools in Toledo, Ohio, proposed a Pizza & a Sub Day for one of his schools. For the highest participation in the United Way Drive, he promised to host a pizza party and to act as a half-day substitute teacher for a lucky winner of a random drawing at their school. In turn, the United Way sponsored an entertaining, motivational speaker to present to all interested district teachers and staff.

We educators are generally givers who don't want to put ourselves in the front. We don't like to appear boastful or self-serving, so we say little about what we do, what we give, and what we give up to do our jobs. It is time for us the teachers to speak up. In an era where just about everyone in this world thinks he or she is an expert on school (just because he or she went to one), it is imperative that those on the frontlines find their collective voice and exercise it.

We should better communicate to our critics that teaching is a craft that must be honed over time. Much of what teachers do to optimize their time with students is invisible to the public eye. And how can we fault them for not knowing about what we all do if we don't tell them?

Educators need to speak out to community groups, the media, and others who influence public opinion to let them know that we want to be accountable, but that many aspects of the positive things we do every single day cannot be measured on a single standardized test. Individually and collectively, we need to focus on those powerful examples of how important we are in the lives of students. We need to do a better job of telling those stories.

As teachers, we plant and sow seeds every day that may not blossom or fully flourish until long after our students have left our classrooms. But the lack of closure does not prevent us from going into our classrooms every day to try and reach every single child. We do it for one reason. We believe it's the right thing to do. We believe that we are making this world a better place and that what we do matters.

We need to support one another, to hold each other accountable, to take care of ourselves, and to speak out in order to elevate our profession. Despite the many paths we took to become teachers, our choice to remain in this profession is generally an act of deliberate optimism, and we need to do everything we can to reclaim our joy in education.

Action Steps for Teachers

DISCUSSION QUESTIONS AND ACTIVITIES

1. How important is salary in hiring and maintaining good teachers? Why do you think that is true? Do other teachers in general agree with your opinion? What about people outside the teaching profession, do they agree with you? Why or why not?

2. Discuss Dina Strasser's list of ways administrators can support teachers. Do you agree with the ones she stated? Did she leave out any that you would like to add?

3. Make a list of ways you think communication can be improved at your school. Prioritize the list by what you think would have the most immediate and greatest impact on morale. Would you or your caucus be willing to share your list with your school leaders? Why or why not?

4. Teachers often complain they are not being treated like professionals. What do they mean by that? How can teachers go about getting that changed?

5. Without violating privacy issues, how can administrators be more transparent in the way they run the school? Are there times that teachers just need to trust their administrators to do the right thing without questioning them? Explain your answer.

6. Do you agree with the authors' assertion that parental involvement is not as much about communication as it is conversation? Defend your answer.

7. List some of the ways you have reached out to parents in the past. How successful were your attempts? Is there something you would like to do that you haven't tried yet (or done for quite some time)? Explain.

8. If you already have student-led conferences at your school, discuss how they could be improved. If you have not yet implemented them, use the questions in the Appendix, page 157, to explore how you could start using them.

9. What ideas can you add to the ones in the chapter for engaging the community with students at your school?

10. In your group, tell at least one story about a difference you made in a student's life. Have you told anyone else that story? Why or why not?

Action Steps for School Leaders

1. Whenever possible, arrange for outstanding teachers to present to community groups such as the Chamber of Commerce, School Board, Rotary Club, Lion's Club, etc., on what is happening at your school. Also make yourself available to local groups to answer questions or accompany students who are making a presentation.

2. Arrange informal parent meetings either at school or at a neutral location (local library, church meeting room, or even the laundromat) for parents with shared interests. If you have non-English-speaking parents, arrange to have a local pastor, a bilingual college student, or some other person who speaks their language to act as an interpreter.

3. Sometimes community members judge a school by its outward appearance. At least every 2 weeks walk around your school and make a detailed visual scan of your campus. Is the marquee sign updated? Are plants pruned and well cared for? Is the parking lot clean? Is the lawn mowed? Are the structures free of graffiti? Students, staff, and community members can be enlisted for a "grounds makeover," if one is needed. Provide tools, gloves, and food.

4. Work with a committee of staff members to ensure that your school is parent-friendly. Signs, posters, and other visuals should help visitors navigate your campus and feel welcome. Discuss with staff and students your expectations for how visitors to the campus will be treated. (You might even have a "secret visitor" much like a "secret shopper" who appears on campus and makes note of each person who is especially friendly or helpful. Those that are noted could receive a small gift card or just a thank-you note from the committee.)

5. Reread Dina Strasser's list of ways administrators can support teachers. Give yourself a letter grade on how well you do on each of the five areas listed. Make a plan on how you will improve an area where your score could be better.

6. On your school website, include a place where staff members, students, parents, and community members can post suggestions for making your school a better place. Allow the posts to be anonymous, if desired, but you will want to screen all posts privately before posting them. Select appropriate comments and questions and respond to them on the website. It is a great way for you to address issues of concerned individuals, to get novel ideas, and to be aware of brewing problems.

7. Create a parent lounge/workroom where parents can meet, create study materials for their children, and relax between volunteer assignments. Get parents to be in charge of the room, coordinate workshops and informal meetings for themselves, and run the volunteer program for your school. Visit often and make a regular "state of our school" presentation and answer any questions they may have.

8. Use the parent portal to its full extent. You can never overcommunicate. Find out each family's preferred mode of communication. Do not assume each house has a computer or even a phone. Share this information with all staff.

9. Make sure that student photos and student work is visible immediately upon entering your building. Let families and visitors know that students are what your school is all about. If you can't paint over the mural from the class of 1991, find another wall for the current class's work.

10. Invite policy makers and community members into your school. Tell them to shadow an educator for just one day. Assure them they will see the best use of tax dollars they have ever witnessed.

Appendix

Life on a Roll

Purpose: To have teachers reflect on why they became teachers and what events brought them to their current positions.

Materials Needed:

- Pencils, pens, markers

- Rulers

- Rolls of paper (similar to receipt machine tape)

Procedure:

1. Give each teacher a long strip of paper. Have them mark off a timeline of their life from beginning to present.

2. Ask each teacher to chronologically note important events in his or her life (good and bad) including those that influenced his or her choice to become a teacher.

3. Allow teachers plenty of time to create their timelines, draw pictures, write words, or otherwise depict their information in a way that best suits them.

4. Tell teachers they do not have to share personal events if they don't want to, but they should mark the proper place on their timelines with a code of some sort to indicate to them when it happened.

5. Either with a partner or in small groups, have participants share their timelines (as much as they are comfortable with) and explain how they ended up where they are now.

(Optional): You can display the timelines for others to see (with or without names on them).

REALISTIC AWARENESS

(Checking the Facts)

Before acting or reacting to news about a challenge or problem, it is helpful to answer the following questions about the information you have.

Describe the mandate, problem, event, or proposal:

1. If the report is about what "they" are doing, who exactly is that? Who is responsible for the decision and/or decision implementation? Be as specific as possible.

2. Have I fact checked the information I have? How thorough was I? How could I learn more?

3. Have I heard more than one side of the issue? Did I give equal weight to differing views? If not, why?

4. Is my conclusion or opinion based on the views of others? Have I considered their possible bias(es) and credibility? Are there limiting factors to accepting their views at face value? What are they?

5. Is it possible my opinion was shaped by my preexisting ideas and conclusions? Did I attribute motives to people's words and/or actions based on my prior beliefs? How fair was I in my judgments?

6. Was there an opportunity for me to give my opinion or to contribute my ideas that I failed to capitalize on?

7. Am I more focused on reacting to the news about this situation than on figuring out a way to make it work? Describe.

8. Have I closely examined any supporting data and taken a hard look at their rationale?

9. Have I made an effort to contact other schools or groups who have tried similar ideas? Explain.

10. Have I reflected on the full potential of this idea (both pros and cons) with a concentration on how it will affect students?

THE FIVE PRINCIPLES OF DELIBERATE OPTIMISM

1. What is the challenge you are dealing with? Explain fully the situation you have and how you feel about what is happening.

2. What steps have you taken to gather as much information as you can about your situation? Where can you go to find further facts and evidence?

3. List the contributing factors that are beyond your control at this time. Explain how you can minimize their impact on your present situation.

4. List all the things you *could* control that would make a positive impact on your situation.

5. Describe the things you are willing to do to at this time to improve your situation. Be specific.

6. What steps could you take, but you do not plan to take at this time? Explain why you are choosing not to control some of the variables that you could.

7. What will be your first step toward improving your situation? When will you do it? Estimate the time it will take you to put your plan into action.

8. When will you review your progress toward your goal? What indicators will you look for in order to know if you are successful or not?

Happiness and Optimism

To get a sense of just how optimistic you are, you can take one or more of the following surveys online:

- **Psychology Today Happiness Test**

  ○ http://psychologytoday.tests.psychtests.com/take_test.php?id RegTest=1320

- **Learned Optimism Test** (adapted from Dr. Martin Seligman's book, *Learned Optimism*)

  ○ http://www.stanford.edu/class/msande271/onlinetools/LearnedOpt. html

- **About.com Optimism Test**

  ○ http://stress.about.com/library/optimismquiz/bl_15optimism_quiz.htm

- *Los Angeles Times* **Optimism Test**

  ○ http://articles.latimes.com/2000/jan/05/news/mn-50931

- You can take a test about your resiliency at **The Resilient Leader Website:**

  ○ http://www.ed.uab.edu/tri/teacherresilienceprofile.asp

The **ProTeacher** social network (www.proteacher.net) is a free online teacher community that has inspirational messages from teachers K–12. On the board, teachers post anecdotes about how they have been inspired, encouraged, or delighted by various positive events during the teaching day. This site has real life stories full of hope and optimism about the teaching profession.

Websites for Getting to Know Ourselves and Each Other

- **Online Gregorc Test** (not the actual one, but close enough)

  o http://www.thelearningweb.net/personalthink.html

- Pretty good test for modalities:

  o http://www.agelesslearner.com/assess/learningstyle.html

- Another good modality test:

  o http://www.personal.psu.edu/bxb11/LSI/LSI.htm

- Lots of different test opportunities of all descriptions:

  o http://www4.uwsp.edu/education/lwilson/links/learningstyles. htm#Learning%20Styles

Ten Tips for Improving Interpersonal Relationships

1. Before you say anything to anyone, ask yourself three things:

   • Is it true?

   • Is it kind?

   • Is it necessary?

2. When people are talking to you, face them and give them your FULL attention. Put aside anything that is distracting you (mobile devices, paperwork, etc.), and concentrate on hearing what they are saying.

3. When people are talking to you, think about understanding what they are saying rather than what you want to reply. Just "taking turns talking" does not lead to healthy communication.

4. If you hear something negative about yourself, consider if there is any truth to it. If there is, fix it. If there isn't, ignore it and trust that the way you live your life will speak for itself.

5. When dealing with a tense conversation, lower your pitch, reduce your volume, and slow the rate of your speech. Remember the adage, "A soft answer turneth away wrath."

6. Refrain from using references to past behaviors to bolster your arguments. As much as possible focus on "the here and now."

7. Remember that it is okay to "agree to disagree." People can strongly disagree on issues but maintain a healthy respect for each other as individuals.

8. Be honest, be specific, and as much as possible, be affirming to others. Never miss an opportunity to let someone know what it is you like about him or her.

9. Remember that laughter is the great equalizer. Always try to maintain a sense of humor about the foibles of other humans.

10. Do not seek so much to be consoled, as to console; do not seek so much to be understood, as to understand; do not seek so much to be loved, as to love. (Prayer of St. Francis)

LOYALTY

Elbert Hubbard

If you work for someone, then work for him: Speak well of him and stand by the institution he represents. Remember, an ounce of loyalty is worth a pound of cleverness. If you must growl, condemn, and eternally find fault, resign your position and when you are on the outside, complain to your heart's content. But as long as you are a part of the institution do not condemn it.

SOURCE: Elbert Hubbard

Effective Team-Building Activities and Icebreakers

MY NAME

In small groups, have each person make a name placard, introduce himself or herself, and tell what he or she knows about why he or she has that particular name. Participants can talk about their first names, middle names, last names, or nicknames.

We have seen some great conversations start with this activity. All kinds of insights are revealed about people's heritage, religion, family, and other seldom talked-about topics.

COMMON ATTRIBUTES

Once participants are arranged in groups, ask one member to be the recorder and write down each individual's name. A group leader should help the members discover 10 (hopefully unusual) things they have in common (e.g., We all have a pierced body part. Each of us has an addiction to chocolate. All of us drive red cars. Everyone's favorite TV show is *Survivor*).

At the end of the icebreaker, one person from each group will introduce each group member and read their group's top five things they have in common. Groups can then vote on whom they thought did the best job of coming up with unusual common attributes. You can award a prize to the group with the most votes.

Pass out a sheet like the one on page 146 to each group.

WHAT I LIKE ABOUT YOU . . .

This is a powerful exercise in helping to build staff morale. Teachers trade papers and respond anonymously with written positive affirmations to colleagues. Often times, secondary teachers will grumble about doing this activity, but don't be surprised if some of them have a major attitude change after participating in this activity. It is worth the effort to make them do it.

Objective: To build a sense of belonging among staff members.

Materials Needed:

- Sheets of paper

List each group member's name:

List your most unusual things in common (they must be true and they must apply to ALL members of the group). When you are finished, put *stars* by your five favorite ones.

Step-by-Step Procedure:

1. Tell the teachers that they are going to get the chance to receive affirmations in a very nonthreatening method.

2. Ask each teacher to put his or her name at the top of a sheet of paper.

3. Collect all the papers and give these directions:

   • "I am going to pass out the papers randomly. When you receive someone's paper think about that person and write something affirming to him or her. You must start your statement with the words *I* or *you*. You cannot use the words *he* or *she*."

   • "When you finish with your message to the person listed at the top of the page, trade papers with someone. Make sure that you never give a paper to the person whose name is at the top. Trade with someone else if you need to."

   • "Please write something different from the other responses on the page. You can affirm the same attribute, but you must phrase it in a different way or give a different example."

   • "Keep trading until I call time."

4. Be sure to participate with the others on this activity. Put your sheet in there, too.

5. At the end of the activity, collect all papers.

6. Ask teachers to express how it felt to write positive affirmations to others. Why was it easier to write to some than to others? (Speak only in a general sense; do not name anyone specifically.)

7. Pass the papers back to their owners and allow participants to read what was written by their colleagues. Ask anyone who would like to share a particularly meaningful comment to do so.

PEOPLE BINGO

People Bingo is one of the most popular icebreakers because it's so easy to customize for your particular group and situation, and everyone knows how to play it. Make your own bingo cards, or use one of the fabulous online card makers.

MAROONED

This icebreaker is a great introduction when people don't know each other, and it fosters team building in groups that already work together. Ask each participant to name the person, who is not a family member, that he or she would want to be stranded with on a deserted island and tell why.

IF I COULDN'T BE AN EDUCATOR

In small groups ask teachers to finish the sentence, "If I could never be a teacher, I would probably want to be a _____." Group members take turns explaining what they would do for a career if they could not have any kind of a job in education and tell why.

School Violence, What Should We Do?

To start the discussion we offer some recent facts about school violence. Please note that the following notes are observations and not meant to stereotype. Also, we ask that you use Step 3 in our Five Principles of Deliberate Optimism, **establish what you can control**, and seek tools and strategies to help you maximize your power, as you explore these findings.

OBSERVATIONS

- Many of the mass shootings are in rural and suburban areas of the country.

- Forty-two percent of the attacks happen in the morning.

- Eighty-two percent of the attackers concealed the weapons and entered the school grounds without issue.

- Most of the shooters are white. Ninety-six percent are males, 62 percent of whom are between the ages of 13 and 19.

- The alleged shooter had easy access to guns in the home or through the Internet.

- Eighty-seven percent of the incidents involved 0–3 fatalities.

- The shooter was detached from the school, and 80 percent were a former or current student of that school.

- The shooter, if school aged, is often described as a loner or had some other issues within the school setting.

- The shooter did not have an adult advocate within the school setting.

SOURCE: Information gathered from Commonwealth Fusion Center—School Shooting Analysis 1992-2012.

TIPS FOR WRITING LETTERS TO STUDENTS

- Write things that are positive and specific to the individual student. (Some students will compare their messages from you to see if you say the same things to everyone.)

- Make sure everyone gets at least one note from you during the year.

- Be truthful and be sincere. You can even be funny if that's how you interact with students, but be very careful that your words cannot be misinterpreted as sarcastic or negative (humor is tricky without the facial expressions and vocal tone to indicate that you are joking).

- Make sure your positive comments have "no strings attached."

- Don't make a big deal of presenting the note. Be as private as possible (you can even leave it in a locker or mail it).

- Don't ask them if they read it; give it freely, and let it go.

- Don't ask for or expect anything in return.

SOURCE: Debbie Silver (2005), *Drumming to the Beat of Different Marchers*, p. 42. Reprinted with permission of the publisher, Incentive Publications by World Book, World Book, Inc., all rights reserved.

How to Listen

1. Stop talking.

2. Imagine the other person's viewpoint.

3. Look, act, and be interested.

4. Don't interrupt.

5. Listen between the lines.

6. Rephrase.

7. Stop talking.

SOURCE: Judith Baenen's workshop, The Difference Between Leaders and Managers

STUDENT ACCOUNTABILITY SHEET

Students can create their own guidelines on how to treat each other and hold each other responsible in class. Here is an example of a student-generated plan:

EXPECTATION

Students will treat each other's property with respect.

AS DEMONSTRATED BY

Breaking something, taking something without permission, or harming someone else's possession.

ACCOUNTABILITY

Student must fix or replace the item. Student must write a letter of apology to the property's owner. Student must do a favor for the property owner.

EXPECTATION

Students will act respectively to each other in and out of class.

AS DEMONSTRATED BY

Taunting, harassing, name-calling, or threatening either in person, by written word, or through cyberspace.

ACCOUNTABILITY

Student will apologize in the same method he or she used to bully a classmate. Student will have conference with the teacher. Student's parents may be notified about the incident.

EXPECTATION

Students will not disrupt the learning process for others.

AS DEMONSTRATED BY

Talking out or over other people, doing something that distracts others, not sharing supplies or responsibilities.

ACCOUNTABILITY

Student will have a "time out" to pay back the time he or she wasted. Student will have to apologize to the class. Student will have to help others to make up for any lost information or time he or she caused them.

STRATEGIES FOR WRITING AWARD-WINNING GRANTS

Debbie Silver

- Make absolutely sure that you have followed ALL rules, regulations, and guidelines! This sounds obvious, but you would be amazed at how many proposals are prescreened and disqualified because of a simple failure to follow directions.

- Have others read and critique your proposal. Let them read it "cold" without any explanation from you. Ask them to make sure that your proposal

  o clearly states a solvable problem,

  o has goals that match those of the sponsor's Request for Proposals (RFP),

  o indicates how the project will benefit students academically,

  o gives a clear purpose for all items that are to be purchased,

  o presents understandable, detailed descriptions of the activities involved,

  o clearly describes how the method of evaluation will measure progress toward the stated purposes and student needs,

  o has a justifiable budget that directly correlates with the objectives of the proposal, and

  o provides solid evidence that you have the skill and experience to successfully implement your plan (special training, workshops, certifications, courses, etc.).

- Be sure you have filled out all required forms and have obtained the required authorization signatures. Check once again to see that your proposal meets each of the requirements on the RFP.

- Send the proposal in a way that can be certified—Express Mail, Federal Express, UPS, or registered mail. Make absolutely certain that your proposal arrives on or before the due date. Late entries are usually discarded unread.

"STUDENT-CENTERED TEACHING"

Debbie Silver

(Student-centered teacher)
(Teacher-centered teacher)

What would you like to learn today?
Read pages one through ten.
Let's look at that another way.
Go do it over ag'in!

Please move into your groups with speed.
Let's get these rows in line.
Feel free to get the things you need.
Touch nothing that is mine!

Brainstorm together on this goal.
No talking, and don't cheat!
To clarify, that is my role.
Don't ask me to repeat!

Please take your time, investigate.
Just copy down these rules!
Try new ideas, initiate.
Don't act like little fools!

Feel free to use the Internet.
You only need your book.
Or any source that you might get.
You don't have long to look!

I'd like to shift your paradigms.
Learn facts, and skip the rest.
Please try to go "outside the lines."
Make sure you pass the test!

I hope that you've enjoyed today.
You've made me lose my mind!
So fun to learn in your own way!
The standards aren't aligned!

Inclusive Versus Excluding Humor

LAUGHING WITH OTHERS	LAUGHING AT OTHERS
1. Going for the jocular vein.	1. Going for the jugular vein.
2. Based on caring and empathy.	2. Based on contempt and insensitivity.
3. Builds confidence.	3. Destroys confidence.
4. Involves people in the fun.	4. Excludes some people.
5. A person enjoys being the "butt" of the joke.	5. A person does not have a choice in being made the "butt" of the joke.
6. Amusing, invites people to laugh.	6. Abusing, offends people.
7. Supportive.	7. Sarcastic.
8. Brings people closer.	8. Divides people.
9. Leads to a positive repartee.	9. Leads to one-man-down-manship cycle.
10. Pokes fun at universal human foibles.	10. Reinforces stereotypes.
11. Nourishing.	11. Toxic.
12. Icebreaker.	12. Ice maker.

SOURCE: Reprinted with permission from Dr. Joel Goodman, Director of The HUMOR Project, Inc. in Saratoga Springs, NY (www.HumorProject.com). Originally appeared in Goodman's *Laughing Matters* magazine.

Some Simple Suggestions for Managing Stress

1. **Talk to someone.** Confide your worry to some levelheaded person you can trust; spouse, parent, friend, clergyman, family doctor, teacher, school counselor. Talking things out often helps you to see things in a clearer light and helps you see what you can do about it.

2. **Be honest in identifying the real source of stress.** Eliminate the source if possible. At least decide on a plan to keep it from getting the best of you.

3. **Accept what you can't control.** Death and taxes are just a few of the things in life you can't avoid. Try to prepare for them as much as possible.

4. **Take good care of yourself.** Eat right. Get enough sleep. Exercise. Learn a relaxation technique. Schedule recreation where you do something for pleasure, something that helps you forget about your work.

5. **Go easy on your criticism.** Don't expect so much of others, and you won't be disappointed. Instead, look for the good in others. You will feel better about yourself.

6. **Shun the "Superwoman" or "Superman" urge.** Don't expect so much of yourself. Nobody is perfect, or capable of doing everything. Decide what you can do well and what you like to do and put your effort into those things.

7. **Do something nice for somebody else.** Then give yourself a pat on the back.

8. **Take ONE THING AT A TIME.** Attack the most urgent tasks—one at a time. Don't overestimate the importance of what you do. Your mental and physical health are vitally important.

9. **Escape for a while.** Making yourself "stand there and suffer" is self-punishment and not a way to solve a problem. Recover your breath and balance, but be prepared to deal with your difficulty when you are composed.

10. **Work off your anger.** If you feel like lashing out at someone, try holding off that impulse for a while. Do something constructive with that energy. Cool down, then handle the problem.

11. **Give in occasionally.** No one is right all of the time. And, even if you are right, it is easier on the system to give in once in a while.

12. **If you need help, get an expert.** These simple suggestions may not be enough to help you handle your stress. If emotional problems become so distressing that you can't cope, you need *professional treatment*, just as you would for any other illness.

STUDENT-LED CONFERENCES

RESOURCES

There are several good resources on student-led conferences that can provide you with more details and information. These are just a few:

- www.educationworld.com/a_admin/admin/admin112.shtml

- www.pbs.org/parents/goingtoschool/student-led-conferences.html

- www.ascd.org/publications/educational_leadership/apr96/vol53/num07/When_Students_Lead_Parent-Teacher_Conferences.aspx

- www.thedailycafe.com/public/471.cfm

QUESTIONS TO ASK BEFORE YOU START

Here are some questions to ask before you venture down the path of student-led conferences. This activity can be used by an individual teacher, an entire team, or the whole staff.

1. What do we hope to accomplish by utilizing student-led conferences? What are our goals for the experience?

2. How can we align class time used for student preparation for student-led conferences with district/state standards and mandated curriculum?

3. What do we need to do to prepare ourselves for the changing from the traditional parent-teacher conferences to student-led? What information and training will we need?

4. Are our students ready for student-led conferences? What training will our students need? How will we begin to get them ready for this next step?

5. How can prepare our parents for the move to student-led conferences? How to we inform them throughout the process?

6. What types of work samples do we need to collect for the conferences?

7. What projects and demonstrations can the students present during the conference?

8. How can we include essentials (encore) teachers in the new conference format?

9. Can we use technology to enhance the conferences and/or reach out to parents who are unable to physically be there?

10. How will we access how well we met our goals? How will we collect data from students and parents after the event?

References

American Institute of Stress. (n.d.). What is stress? Retrieved from http://www.stress.org/ what-is-stress/#sthash.ZbZ86U2Z.dpuf

Azzam, A. M. (2013). Handle with care. A conversation with Maya Angelou. *Educational Leadership, 71*(1), 10–13.

Bainbridge, C. (2014). Introvert. Retrieved from http://giftedkids.about.com/od/glossary/g/ introvert.htm

Bandura, A. (1986). *Social foundations of thought and action: A social-cognitive theory.* Englewood Cliffs, NJ: Prentice Hall.

Bandura, A. (1997). *Self-efficacy: The exercise of control.* New York, NY: Worth Publishers.

Bandura, A. (2009). Cultivate self-efficacy for personal and organizational effectiveness. In E. A. Locke (Ed.), *Handbook of principles of organization behavior* (2nd ed., pp. 179–200). New York, NY: Wiley.

Berckemeyer, J. C. (2012). *Taming of the team: How great teams work together.* Chicago, IL: Incentive by World Book, Inc.

Berckemeyer, J. C. (2013). Why Johnny can't sing, dance, saw, or bake. Retrieved from http:// www.amle.org/BrowsebyTopic/Curriculum/CurrDet/TabId/186/ArtMID/793/ ArticleID/367/Why-Johnny-Cant-Sing-Dance-Saw-or-Bake.aspx

Bielski, Z. (2012). Despite overprograming, kids today have bigger imaginations than previous generations: Study. *Globe and Mail.* Retrieved from http://www.theglobeandmail .com/life/parenting/young-children/children-development/despite-overprogram ming-kids-today-have-bigger-imaginations-than-previous-generations-study/ article2448839/?utm_medium=Feeds%253A%20RSS%252FAtom&utm_ source=Life&utm_content=2448839

Brassell, D. (2012). *Bringing joy back into the classroom.* Huntington Beach, CA: Shell Educational Publishing.

Bronson, P. (2010). The creativity crisis. *Newsweek.* Retrieved from www.huffingtonpost .com/2010/07/10/the-creativity-crisis-in_n_641790.html

Brown, B. (2010). *The gifts of imperfection: Let go of who you think you're supposed to be and embrace who you are.* Center City, MN: Hazelden Publishing.

Brown, B. (2013). *Daring greatly: How the courage to be vulnerable transforms the way we live, love, parent, and lead.* New York, NY: Gotham.

Bryant, Charles W. (2008). Is sleep that important? *HowStuffWorks.com.* Retrieved from http://health.howstuffworks.com/mental-health/sleep/basics/importance-of-sleep .htm

Buyse, E., Verschueren, K., Verachtert, P., & Van Damme, J. (2009). Predicting school adjustment in early elementary school: Impact of teacher-child relationship quality and relational classroom climate. *Elementary School Journal, 110*(2), 119–141. Retrieved from http://dx.doi.org/10.1086/605768

Cain, S. (2012). *Quiet: The power of introverts in a world that won't stop talking.* New York, NY: Crown Publishing Company.

CommonWealth Fusion Center, Massachusetts State Police, Infrastructure Protection-Information Center. (2012). Retrieved from www.state.nj.us/education/schools/security/threats/AnalysisofSchoolShootings.pdf

Connolly, M. R. (2013). Educators must be prepared to challenge politicians and business leaders' education agenda. Retrieved from http://michaelrconnollyjr.weebly.com/1/post/2013/05/educators-must-be-prepared-to-challenge-politicians-and-business-leaders-education-agenda.html

Connors, N. A. (2000). *If you don't feed the teacher they eat the students: Guide to success for administrators and teachers.* Nashville, TN: Incentive Publications.

Curwin, R. (2013). Cynicism is contagious; so is hope. *Edutopia.* Retrieved from http://www.edutopia.org/blog/cynicism-is-contagious-richard-curwin

Deci, E. L., & Ryan, R. M. (2000). The "what" and "why" of goal pursuits: Human needs and the self-determination of behavior. *Psychological Inquiry, 11,* 227–268.

Dogru, M., & Kalender, S. (2007). Applying the subject "cell" through constructionist approach during science lessons and the teacher's view. *International Journal of Science Education, 2*(1), 3–13.

Elden, R. (2011). *See me after class: Advice for teachers by teachers* (2nd ed.). Naperville, IL: Sourcebooks.

Elliot-Yeary, S. (2011). *Ties to tattoos: Turning generational differences into a competitive advantage.* Dallas, TX: Brown Publishing Company.

Employee job satisfaction and engagement: A research report by SHRM, 2011. (2011). Retrieved from http://www.shrm.org/research/surveyfindings/articles/documents/11-0618%20job_satisfaction_fnl.pdf

Esquith, R. (2014). Can't wait for Monday. *Educational Leadership, 71*(5), 20–22.

Ferlazzo, L. (2013). Response: Recover from bad days by seeing "disasters as opportunities." *Education Week Teacher.* Retrieved from http://blogs.edweek.org/teachers/classroom_qa_with_larry_ferlazzo/2013/11/response_recover_from_a_bad_day_by_seeing_disasters_as_opportunities.html

Gallup Poll on Education. (2013). Retrieved from www.gallup.com

Gregorc, A. F. (1982). *An adult's guide to style.* Columbia, CT: Gregorc Associates.

Gregorc, A. F. (1984). Style as a symptom: A phenomenological perspective. *Theory Into Practice, 23*(1), 51–55.

Gregorc, A. F. (n.d.). Mind styles. Retrieved from http://www.web.cortland.edu/andersmd/learning/gregorc.htm

Groening, M. (2004). *School is hell.* New York, NY: HarperCollins Entertainment.

Goodman, J. (n.d.). The Humor Project, Inc. Retrieved from www.HumorProject.com

Hallowell, E. (2007). *Crazy busy.* New York, NY: Ballantine Books.

Hargraeaves, A., & Fullan, M. (2013). The power of professional capital: With an investment in collaboration, teachers become nation builders. *Journal of Staff Development (JSD), 34*(3), 36–39.

Heaner, M. (2004, October 12). Snooze alarm takes its toll on a nation. *New York Times.* Retrieved from http://www.nytimes.com/2004/10/12/health/12snoo.html?pagewanted=all&position=#

Henderson, N. (2013). Havens of resilience. *Educational Leadership, 71*(1), 22–27.

Henson, J. (2005). *It's not easy being green.* New York, NY: Hyperion.

Hetlin, L. (2012). National teacher of the year: Give us a career path. *Education Week Teacher.* Retrieved from http://www.edweek.org/tm/articles/2012/10/17/tl_mieli wocki.html

How to keep good teachers motivated. (n.d.). *Education World.* Retrieved from http://www .educationworld.com/a_admin/admin/admin289.shtml

Ingersoll, R. (2012). Beginning teacher induction: What the data tell us. *Kappan, 93*(8), 47–51.

Kim, K. H. (2011). The creativity crisis: The decrease in creative thinking scores on the Torrance tests of creative thinking. *Creativity Research Journal, 23*(4), 285–295.

Larkin, D. B. (2013). 10 things to know about mentoring student teachers. *Kappan, 49*(7), 28–43.

Lemov, D. (2010). *Teach like a champion.* San Francisco, CA: Josey-Bass Publishers.

Magaña, S., & Marzano, R. (2013). *Enhancing the art & science of teaching with technology.* Denver, CO: Marzano Research Lab.

Mandela, N. (1995). *Long walk to freedom: Autobiography of Nelson Mandela.* New York, NY: Back Bay Books.

McCarthy, C. J., Lambert, R. G., O'Donnel, M., & Melendres, L. T. (2009). The relation of elementary teachers' experience, stress, and coping resources to burnout symptoms. *Elementary School Journal, 109*(3), 282–300.

Music Education Online. (n.d.). Why music? Retrieved from http://elecqlx.sasktelweb hosting.com/links/why.html

Nelson, S. (2013). *Teaching: The most noble profession.* Retrieved from http://www.huffing tonpost.com/steve-nelson/teaching-the-most-noble-p_b_2471894.html

Noddings, N. (2014). High morale in a good cause. *Educational Leadership, 71*(5), 15–18.

Notter, J. (2013, March 6). Conflict and generations in the workplace. Online journal for The American Society of Training and Development. Retrieved from http://www .astd.org/Publications/Blogs/Workforce-Development-Blog/2013/03/ Conflict-and-Generations-in-the-Workplace

Plachetka, B. (2014). *A systems approach to workplace bullying in the K–12 public educational setting.* Doctoral dissertation (in press), Aurora University, Aurora, IL.

Richardson, J. (2013). Wanted: Highly effective teachers. *Kappan, 94*(7), 4.

Rockwell, D. (2013). 10 ways to "deal with" quiet people. *Leadership Freak Blog,* February. Retrieved from http://leadershipfreak.wordpress.com/2013/02/05/10-ways-to-deal-with-quiet-people/

Rubenstein, J. S., Meyer, D.E., & Evans, J. E. (2001). Executive control of cognitive pro-cesses in task switching. *Journal of Experimental Psychology: Human Perception and Per-formance, 27*(4), 763–797.

Ryan, R. M., & Deci, E. L. (2000). Self-determination and the facilitation of intrinsic motivation, social development and well-being. *American Psychologist, 55*, 68–78.

Seligman, M. E. P. (2006). *Learned optimism: How to change your mind and your life.* New York, NY: Vintage Books.

Seligman, M. E. P., & Maier, S. F. (1967). Failure to escape traumatic shock. *Journal of Experimental Psychology, 74*(1), 1–9.

Silver, D. (2005). *Drumming to the beat of different marchers.* Chicago, IL: Incentive by World Book, Inc.

Silver, D. (2013a). *Fall down 7 times, get up 8: Teaching kids to succeed.* Thousand Oaks, CA: Corwin.

Silver, D. (2013b). Relax and recharge: 5 ways to de-stress this summer. *The Classroom Teacher, 34*(2), 18.

Silver, D. (2014). Freedom to fall and get up and succeed. *Principal Leadership, 14*(5), 48–51.

Stafford, D. (n.d.). *Reach to teach blog.* Retrieved from http://www.dedrastafford.com

Strasser, D. (2014). An open letter on teacher morale. *Educational Leadership, 71*(5), 10–13.

Strobel, J., & van Barneveld, A. (2009). When is PBL more effective? A meta-synthesis of meta-analyses comparing PBL to conventional classrooms. *The Interdisciplinary Journal of Problem-Based Learning, 3*(1).

Van Dongen, H., Maisliln, G., Mullington, J. M., & Dinges, D. F. (2003).The cumulative cost of additional wakefulness: Dose-response effects on neurobehavioral function and sleep physiology from chronic sleep restriction and total sleep deprivation. *SLEEP, 26*(2), 117–126.

Walker, A., & Leary, H. (2009). A problem-based learning meta-analysis: Differences across problem types, implementation types, disciplines, and assessment levels. *Interdisciplinary Journal of Problem-Based Learning, 3*(1), 12–43.

Wolpert-Gawron, H. (2013). Teachers: Staying positive in trying times. *Edutopia.* Retrieved from http://www.edutopia.org/blog/teaching-staying-positive-trying-time-heather-wolpert-gawron

Workplace Bullying Institute (WBI). (n.d.). Retrieved from http://www.workplacebullying.org/individuals/problem/definition/

Zappos Company. (n.d.). Retrieved from http://about.zappos.com/our-unique-culture/zappos-core-values/be-passionate-and-determined

Index

quest-based learning and, 98
student self-monitoring/self-discipline and, 99, 100
technology, integration of, 97–98, 99
See also Joyful school communities; Life-work balance; Optimistic classrooms

Khan Academy, 97, 98
Kim, K. H., 91
Koepke, D., 54
Kuralt, C., 121, 122

Larkin, D. B., 63
Layering tasks, 109
Leadership. *See* Deliberate optimism; Education; School leadership
Learned helplessness, 22–23
Learned optimism, 23, 33
    ABC Method of, 23–25
    ABCD Model and, 25–26
    ABCDE Model and, 26–27, 31
    See also Optimism skill development
Learned Optimism Test, 141
Learning centers, 98–100
Learning styles, 38–40
    abstract random learners and, 41–42
    abstract sequential learners and, 42–43
    abstract thinking and, 39
    concrete random learners and, 43–44
    concrete sequential learners and, 40–41
    concrete thinking and, 39
    Gregorc Style Delineator and, 44
    measurement instruments for, 44, 142
    Mind Styles Model and, 38, 44
    ordering ability and, 39–40
    perceptual qualities and, 39
    project-based learning and, 92–93
    random/chunked ordering and, 39–40
    sequential/linear ordering and, 39
    See also Negative behavior patterns
Lemov, D., 74
Letter writing, 76, 150
Life on a Roll activity, 138
Life-work balance, 105
    action steps for, 119–120
    attentive focus and, 109
    body signals and, 107–108
    burnout risk and, 105, 108
    collegial relationships and, 117
    commitments, control over, 110–112
    exercise programs and, 114–115
    friend, definition of, 117
    help-seeking and, 118
    humor, role of, 106–107, 155
    hydration, attention to, 114
    inclusive vs. exclusive humor and, 107, 155
    joy, experience of, 108
    layered tasks and, 109
    mental well-being, maintenance of, 118
    mindfulness, cultivation of, 118
    multitasking, myth of, 108–109
    nutritional care and, 112–113, 114

overstimulation, effects of, 109
    personal bodily needs and, 113
    physical well-being, stress and, 107
    proactive medical check-ups and, 117
    relaxation, scheduling of, 117–118
    self-care and, 105–106, 108
    single-tasking and, 110
    sleep hygiene and, 115–116
    stress indicators and, 106
    stress management strategies and, 156
    volunteer opportunities and, 110–112
    wellness programs and, 113
    See also Joyful school communities; Joyful teaching
Listening skills, 80, 151
Los Angeles Times Optimism Test, 141
Loyalty, 144

Maier, S. F., 23
Maisliln, G., 115
Mandela, N., 21
Marooned activity, 148
Meyer, D. E., 109
Mieliwocki, R., 59
Millennials, 47, 49, 97
Mind Styles Model, 38, 44
Mindfulness, 118
Mini-courses, 96–97
Moral calling, 3, 5
Motivation theory, 28
Mullington, J. M., 115
Multiple intelligences (M.I.), 6, 99
Multitasking, 108–109
The Music Achievements Council, 95
Music education, 95
My Name activity, 145

National Association of Secondary School Principals (NASSP), 60
National Inventors Hall of Fame School, 91
Negative behavior patterns, 37–38
    action steps for, 50–52
    bullying behaviors and, 56–58, 59
    controllable circumstances, determination of, 58–60
    deliberate optimism principles and, 38
    extroverts/introverts and, 44–46
    generational differences and, 46–49
    learning styles and, 38–44
    negative impacts, minimization of, 54–56
    relationship building and, 54
    supervisory personnel and, 57
    talking snakes, avoidance of, 55–56
    See also Deliberate optimism; Optimism skill development; Optimistic shared community
Nelson, S., 17
Niehuhr, R., 10
No Child Left Behind (NCLB) Act of 2001, 9
Noddings, N., 29
Nooter, J., 49

Online Gregorc Test, 142
Optimism measurement, 141

A SAGE Company

Corwin is committed to improving education for all learners by publishing books and other professional developmentresources for those serving the field of PreK–12 education. By providing practical, hands-on materials, Corwin continues to carry out the promise of its motto: **"Helping Educators Do Their Work Better."**